THE
SOUTH
BEACH
DIET
Parties & Holidays
Cookbook

THE SOUTH BEACH DIET

Parties & Holidays Cookbook

HEALTHY RECIPES FOR ENTERTAINING FAMILY AND FRIENDS

Arthur Agatston, MD

Author of the #1 *New York Times* Bestseller *The South Beach Diet*

RODALE®

© 2006 by Arthur Agatston, MD
The South Beach Diet® is a Registered Trademark of the SBD Trademark Limited Partnership.

Printed in the United States of America
Rodale Inc. makes every effort to use acid-free ♾, recycled paper ♲.

Book design by Carol Angstadt
Photography by Mitch Mandel
Food styling by Diane Simone Vezza
Prop styling by Melissa DeMayo
Prop styling on pages 32 and 186 by Francine Matalon-Degni

Library of Congress Cataloging-in-Publication Data

Agatston, Arthur.
    The South Beach diet parties & holidays cookbook : healthy recipes for entertaining family and friends / Arthur Agatston.
        p.   cm.
    Includes index.
    ISBN-13: 978–1–59486–444–5   paperback
    ISBN-10: 1–59486–444–6   paperback
    1. Reducing diets—Recipes. 2. Weight loss. 3. Holiday cookery. 4. Parties. I. Title.
II. Title: South Beach diet parties and holidays cookbook.
RM222.2.A3494   2006
641.5'635—dc22   2006016182

Distributed to the trade by Holtzbrinck Publishers

2   4   6   8   10   9   7   5   3   1   paperback

To our siblings, cousins, aunts, and uncles

with whom we share the joys of celebration.

And, as always, to my wife, Sari.

CONTENTS

Holidays

ACKNOWLEDGMENTS

The South Beach Diet Parties & Holidays Cookbook is our sixth book with Rodale, and there are many people to credit for helping us in our continuing mission to change the way America eats. In particular I would like to thank Liz Perl, Margot Schupf, and Cindy Ratzlaff for their enthusiasm and support, and my editor, Marya Dalrymple, for her "party-on" spirit and advice.

I would also like to especially thank Rodale's art director Carol Angstadt, whose vision and hard work have made this book so beautiful. In addition Nancy N. Bailey, JoAnn Brader, Mitch Mandel, and Diane Vezza all contributed many hours of their time to the project.

Special credit goes to Mindy Fox, who developed the delicious and healthy party and holiday menus and recipes, and to Marie Almon, my nutrition director, who helped to set the high standards for the book.

I am also grateful to Margo Lowry of the South Beach Diet partnership for her continual wisdom and support and to Thomas Connell, executive chef of the Ritz-Carlton hotel in South Beach, for helping to bring the important message of this book to the public.

Finally, I would like to thank my wife, best friend, and main advisor, Sari, and my sons, Evan and Adam, for helping me celebrate life not just on special occasions, but everyday.

INTRODUCTION

No matter what the time of year, there's always something to celebrate—from religious and national holidays to birthdays, anniversaries, and successes of all sorts. And there's no better way to mark these special occasions than to get together with friends and family and share a memorable meal.

Recently our family did just that to celebrate my son's 18th birthday. It was a wonderful evening spent laughing and reminiscing over a delicious dinner. At the end of the meal, there was, naturally, birthday cake (a sinful, sugar- and fat-laden, empty-calorie confection!). I follow the South Beach Diet lifestyle, too, of course, but I did have a small piece of that cake in honor of my son—and loved every bite of it. I felt a little guilty afterward, but that feeling didn't last long. Who knows better than I that a great dessert can—and should—be an occasional part of a good meal, especially when the rest of the meal is filled with nutritious choices? So rather than spend time fretting over a dessert that I truly enjoyed, I simply resumed my normal healthy eating habits the next day and got back to my exercise program.

If you're already leading a South Beach Diet lifestyle, you know what I'm talking about. You know that you can count on the South Beach Diet philosophy to help you make good food selections, whatever the occasion. And when you do occasionally have that special treat, you can always count on the diet to help you get back on track.

Enjoy Healthy Eating Every Day

Thankfully, the confusion that has characterized diet advice for so many years is over. We have moved beyond the low-fat versus low-carb debates to a broad consensus of expert opinion regarding the principles of healthy eating. These principles are simple: Choose good, unsaturated fats (such as olive oil, canola oil, and omega-3 fish oils); nutrition-rich, high-fiber carbohydrates; lean sources of protein; and low-fat dairy. While there is certainly more to learn about the nutrient benefits of various foods, these basic tenets will not change. They are, in fact, the principles that form the basis of the South Beach Diet and lifestyle.

Now that there is finally agreement on the fundamentals of good eating, our challenge is to apply this knowledge in our daily lives. With each of our South Beach Diet cookbooks, we have demonstrated that healthy eating is consistent with a wide range of wonderful tasting dishes that can be prepared quickly and easily. With our shopping and dining guides, we've shown that it is possible to make the right food and meal choices—anytime, anywhere.

With *The South Beach Diet Parties & Holidays Cookbook,* we embrace another significant area of our food culture—preparing memorable meals for special occasions throughout the year. Whether you're throwing a Super Bowl party, enjoying a romantic Valentine's Day dinner, or hosting an Easter brunch, a Passover Seder, a Thanksgiving feast, or a barbecue in the backyard, all of the menus and recipes in this book prove that delicious party and holiday fare fits right in with the sound eating principles of the South Beach Diet. And that means enjoying the occasional dessert, too. If you turn to page 143, you'll see that I've even managed to include one of my personal favorites—a decadent chocolate torte with a rich ganache glaze.

Some Practical Advice

Many of my friends and patients have asked me for tips on practicing the South Beach Diet lifestyle during parties and holidays. The advice I give them may seem almost too simple, but I can tell you it works: Don't abandon your regular South Beach Diet principles.

What I mean is that on party day you'll eat the same healthy foods you always do on the South Beach Diet and get some exercise as well. This will help you manage your hunger and avoid going overboard during the event. For example, if you're already following our lifestyle, you know that a great day begins with a good breakfast. This might include a protein choice, like a cheese and veggie omelet, or a low-fat dairy choice, such as a fruit and yogurt parfait. A couple of hours later, you may feel hungry again. That's when it's time to reach for a nutritious snack, like some nuts, a few slices of low-fat cheese or turkey, or some veggies and hummus. These types of snacks will fill you up while simultaneously working to prevent a drop in your blood sugar.

As you may already know from reading my other books, if you don't keep your blood sugar stable by eating slowly digested, nutrient-dense, fiber-rich meals and snacks at regular times during the day, you may experience cravings. These are brought on by reactive hypoglycemia—a cycle that begins when your brain detects too-low blood sugar and your body responds by craving sugary carbohydrates to raise it. Once you get caught in this cycle (one that puts you at risk not only for weight gain but also for diabetes and other diseases), your cravings will only get worse as you gain belly fat. Phase 1 of the South Beach Diet is designed to break this cycle.

In fact, you actually put yourself in a difficult position if you "prepare" for a special occasion by eating less than you normally do during the day—or, worse yet, nothing at all—just so you can have more food at the party later on. When you're running on empty like this, your blood sugar drops significantly, and the next thing you know, you'll be diving into those canapés or Christmas cookies with reckless abandon. If, on the other hand, you keep eating well throughout the day—as you normally do—you won't arrive at the party or holiday meal feeling ravenous. As a result, you'll be better able to make the best choices throughout the meal—including having a glass of wine or two and a taste of something sweet—and come away from the table feeling very satisfied.

A Few Specifics about the South Beach Diet

If you're already following the South Beach Diet, you know that it's divided into three phases. You also know how much better you look and feel because you're eating so well. You've mastered your cravings and are on your way to making good food choices for life. If you're new to the diet, welcome! Here's a quick summary of how it works.

Phase 1: This is the shortest phase of the diet, lasting only 2 weeks. Phase 1 is for people who have significant cravings for refined starches and sugar or who have a substantial amount of weight to lose. The purpose of this phase is to stabilize blood-sugar levels to minimize those cravings. During this time, you'll eat plenty of healthy foods, including lean protein (fish, chicken, and lean cuts of beef), high-fiber vegetables, nuts, reduced-fat cheeses, eggs, low-fat dairy, and good unsaturated fats, such as olive oil and canola oil. You'll eat three meals a day and at least two snacks. And you'll even be able to have some desserts, too! What you won't be eating are starches, including pasta, rice, and bread of any type. And you'll also eliminate sugar, which means no fruits or fruit juices. While this may sound difficult, these simple adjustments to your diet will kick-start your weight loss, improve your blood chemistry, and reduce cravings. And, in just 2 short weeks, you'll be adding these foods back into your life.

Phase 2: Those people who have 10 pounds or less to lose, who don't have problems with cravings, or who simply want to improve their health, can start the diet with Phase 2. If you're moving onto Phase 2 from Phase 1, you'll find that your weight will continue to steadily drop and your cravings will have subsided. On Phase 2, you will gradually reintroduce many of the foods that were off-limits on Phase 1, including good carbs such as whole-grain breads, whole-wheat pasta, and brown rice, as well as whole fruits and some root vegetables (such as sweet potatoes). You will also be able to have a glass or two of red or white wine with meals, if you like. You will continue on Phase 2 until you reach a weight that's healthy for you.

Phase 3: This phase begins once you reach your healthy weight. You'll continue to choose the right carbs, the right fats, lean sources of protein, and plenty of fiber. At this point, you'll fully understand how to eat while maintaining your health and your weight. Because your South Beach Diet lifestyle will be second nature and you'll be able to monitor your body's response to particular foods with ease, you'll find yourself naturally making the right choices and enjoying foods of all types—whether you're cooking at home for yourself and your family, dining out, throwing a great party, or celebrating a holiday.

A Word about Dieting during the Holidays

If you're already on Phase 2 or Phase 3 of the South Beach Diet, I suggest that you continue to follow its healthy eating principles throughout the holiday season. That way you won't face weight gain and feel bad once the holidays are over.

Don't Forget to Exercise

Exercise is an essential component of the South Beach Diet and one that shouldn't be forgotten at party and holiday time. Not only does regular exercise help you lose weight faster and sustain that weight loss, it also lowers your risk for virtually all diseases and chronic health problems. In addition, a good workout can boost mood-elevating hormones called endorphins (a boon if you're a stressed-out host).

I recommend getting at least 30 minutes of brisk aerobic activity plus at least 10 to 15 minutes of stretching and resistance exercise on most days. When that isn't possible, try to at least work in a 10-minute walk. You'll find that exercise will both relax and invigorate you, and you'll fully enjoy the rest of your day.

I don't suggest beginning Phase 1 right before or during the holidays. Instead, focus on the healthy-eating principles recommended in Phase 2 and Phase 3 during the busy holiday season. One good way to do that is to prepare many of the nutritious recipes we've included in this and our other South Beach Diet cookbooks. Then, if necessary, you can begin Phase 1 (or Phase 2) of the South Beach Diet at the start of the new year. Have some friends join you for a Phase 1 Kickoff Party (see pages 13 to 21). At the party, solidify your diet commitments, make a pact to help each other through the 2 weeks of Phase 1, and share your best dieting strategies.

Remember, the South Beach Diet is about living well. As you get together with family and friends to celebrate festive occasions throughout the year, relax, have a great time, and enjoy preparing and eating these delicious and nutritious meals.

ARTHUR AGATSTON, MD

HEALTHY ENTERTAINING ON THE SOUTH BEACH DIET

You may think that you have to shop and cook differently than you usually do on the South Beach Diet in order to throw a memorable party. But just the opposite is true. As you prepare the recipes in this book, you'll realize that making dishes for special occasions means using the same nutritious ingredients that you choose on a day-to-day basis. From tantalizing appetizers to sumptuous desserts, you'll be producing fantastic, healthy meals that will remain in your entertaining repertoire for years to come.

In fact, if you love to cook classic dishes for festive occasions, you'll find yourself continually turning to this book. Our Christmas Day menu, for example, features a mouthwatering Crown Roast of Pork served with Apple-Onion Chutney, tender Braised Red Cabbage, and nutty Green Beans Amandine (see pages 217 to 231). Our healthy Easter menu puts a lemony Spring Quinoa Salad alongside a traditional Herb and Garlic Roasted Leg of Lamb (see pages 145 to 153). And for the Fourth of July, there are fantastic Firecracker Cheddar Burgers (page 179) made with lean ground beef and reduced-fat cheese.

And who could throw a Super Bowl party without a great chili or have Thanksgiving without turkey, stuffing, and pumpkin pie? We've updated these must-haves without ever compromising taste. So, when you host your South Beach Diet Super Bowl Bash, you'll serve a hearty Pork and Poblano Chili (page 56) made with a lean cut of meat and loads of nutritious, fiber-rich vegetables and beans. And for Thanksgiving, you'll make a Pumpkin Pie (page 194) that has all the creamy sweetness and spice you'd expect, plus a

1

delicate, buttery-tasting phyllo crust in place of one made with white flour, sugar, and butter.

We've also included plenty of dishes in every menu for vegetarian guests, as well as recipes that will appeal to kids. And to complement some of the meals, we've come up with some unique mocktails—thirst-quenching, non-alcoholic drinks like Pomegranate Punch (page 123) and Mint-Ginger Spritzers (page 153)—that can be used interchangeably from one party to another.

Finally, no party or holiday meal would be complete without dessert: Your guests expect it, and of course you'll want to enjoy a few bites yourself. For this reason, we've continued to use the healthiest ingredients to make all the desserts in this book. We've included old favorites, like a warm Blueberry Cobbler (page 87) for our Backyard Grill Fest, as well as new ideas like refreshing Lemon-Thyme Ices (page 175) for Mother's Day and some adorable mini Boy or Girl Angel Cakes (page 41) that are perfect for a baby shower.

Bottom line: By using the healthy foods and cooking techniques we recommend throughout this book, you will be able to enjoy your South Beach Diet lifestyle at any party you throw. And as an added bonus, you'll feel better knowing that you're staying healthy.

How to Use This Book

Before you jump in and start cooking, there are a few things we want you to know about the organization of this book and its special features.

We've divided the book into two main sections. The first part features 10 festive parties, ranging from a Phase 1 Kickoff to celebrate your new lifestyle (and ideally help some friends start the diet, too) to a Rite of Passage Party to ring in a milestone event. Some of the parties are seasonal, like the Super Bowl Bash, and others, like the Family Buffet, can be held at anytime of the year. Many of the parties can easily be adapted to suit a wide variety of occasions. For example, you can host the Hors d'Oeuvres for a Crowd party to celebrate a new job or an engagement or throw the Backyard Grill Fest or Weekend Brunch for a birthday or graduation party. The Baby Shower can be easily modified to fit a wedding shower.

The second part of the book features 11 holidays that fall throughout the year, from New Year's Day to Christmas Day. We've included traditional occasions, such as Passover, Easter, Cinco de Mayo, and Thanksgiving, as well as menus for other celebrations like Valentine's Day and Mother's Day.

On the opening page for each party and holiday, you'll find a Game Plan—a quick reference tool that helps you get and stay organized. It lets you see at a glance which dishes can be prepared ahead and reminds you when to order special items in advance, like the crown roast of pork for Christmas. The Game Plans start as early as a month ahead (when certain dishes can be prepared and frozen) and lead you right up to what has to be done on the day of the party. Remember that you don't have to follow the Game Plans or the full menu for any event. Set up a schedule that works best for you, and leave out a soup course or an appetizer if time is tight or if you prefer to make less food.

White Wine, White Flour

Occasionally we've used ingredients in this book that are on the "Foods to Avoid" list for a particular phase or for the diet in general. For example, in the Roast Turkey with Fresh Herbs recipe (page 188) and the Steamed Mussels recipe (page 71), we use a little white wine. Because most of the wine evaporates during cooking, this small amount is fine for flavoring these Phase 1 recipes. In certain Phase 3 recipes, such as the Almond Star Cookies (page 184) and the Orange-Pecan Scones (page 46), we have added some white flour along with whole-grain pastry flour to improve the texture of these baked goods. Our goal is to make these recipes tasty and better for you. If you follow the nutritional principles of the South Beach Diet, having a little white wine or white flour in a recipe on occasion should have no lasting effect on your weight loss or overall health goals.

Each of the Game Plans works in tandem with the Make-Ahead instructions that appear beneath most of the recipes in this book. If you're following all or part of the Game Plan, you'll want to look to the Make-Ahead information for specific details. For example, if you choose to prepare the Chicken Cassoulet (page 73) ahead of time for the French Bistro Party, you'll turn to its Make-Ahead information for instructions on how to store the dish once it's cooked and how to reheat it on party day.

And to help you plan ahead even further, we've also provided prep and cook times with each recipe. While many of the recipes can be done on the day of the party, others may involve freezing or overnight marinating or a special technique that might require a little extra effort. You'll want to pay attention to these times as you plan your menus.

In addition, each recipe is marked with the appropriate phase. If you're on Phase 1 and want to throw one of the parties that include Phase 2 and Phase 3 dishes, you can substitute Phase 1 dishes from other menus to create your own Phase 1 party. Of course, if you're on Phase 2 or Phase 3, you can prepare the Phase 1 recipes anytime.

Following each recipe, you'll find "Nutrition at a Glance." This breakdown will give you the calories, total fat and saturated fat, protein, carbohydrate, cholesterol, and fiber in an individual serving, and it can also help you keep track of sodium, if it's a concern. Remember, this is a special-occasion cookbook, so you'll intentionally be preparing more food than you normally do for an average meal on an average day. In fact, many of the recipes do provide seconds for those guests who might want an extra serving. And some menus may feature more than one entrée or more than one dessert so you can easily feed a crowd. For every recipe, we've indicated the number of servings and serving sizes (for example, 3 canapés, 1 cookie, 1 cup soup) where useful, to help guide you as you make these nutritious dishes.

Planning a Great South Beach Diet Party

From the time you make the decision to host a party to the moment you see your last guest out the door, there are all kinds of things to consider. (See our

"Checklist for Success" on pages 8 and 9.) Each party you give will have its own special flair, but you'll find these general pointers useful, too.

First decide what type of party you want to have and how many people you'd like to include. Our parties and holidays range in size from 2 guests to 12, but you can easily scale them up or down for larger or smaller groups. Just double or triple the recipes to accommodate more people or cut the recipes by half if you invite fewer guests.

Think about what kind of atmosphere your home has or what feeling you want to create. Will your party be formal or laid-back? Held indoors or out? Be an afternoon or an evening event?

Choose a serving style. For example, the Rite of Passage Party and New Year's Day Open House work particularly well as buffet-style events. The Easter Gathering and Thanksgiving can be served family-style. And the Valentine's Day Dinner for 2 and Mother's Day Luncheon make more intimate meals. There's plenty of flexibility here, so decide what works best for you.

Consider who's coming. Is your party just for adults, or will there be children invited, too? Our Fourth of July Revel and Family Buffet include a lot of kid-friendly food choices, while the French Bistro Party pleases more sophisticated palates.

Pick a theme. Cinco de Mayo is a fun one to try. You can enhance the theme of a party like this by making maraca-shaped invitations, playing Mexican music, or having guests swing at a piñata. The Super Bowl Bash and Fourth of July Revel also make great theme-oriented occasions.

Enjoying Party Day the South Beach Diet Way

You've planned, sent invites, shopped, and cooked. Now party day is finally here. You may be feeling a little stressed, but you don't have to be. The following suggestions can help you stay energized and worry-free before, during, and after the event.

Don't change your normal eating routine. As mentioned earlier, on the days leading up to the party, and especially on the day of, stick to whatever phase of the diet you're on and make sure to eat breakfast, lunch, and healthy snacks. This way, you won't be hungry while you're preparing the party food, and when the party starts, you won't be famished.

Keep yourself hydrated. While you don't need to keep an exact count of how many glasses of water you consume on a daily basis, being well hydrated will help you stay energized and combat headaches and fatigue—two things you want to avoid on party day. Drink water when you feel thirsty and remember that fruits, vegetables, and milk contribute to your water intake.

Schedule time for exercise. Getting some exercise decreases stress and increases energy. When you exercise, your body releases feel-good hormones called endorphins, which help relieve stress and keep your blood sugar levels stable so that you don't get cravings. If it's too hard to work in an aerobics, Pilates, or yoga class on party day, take a brisk walk or go for a bike ride or a swim.

Enlist friends to help. We all have friends or family members who want to aid with party and holiday meals. Saying yes to a little assistance is a great way to reduce stress. Have your volunteers arrive early to prep a dish or two, arrange flowers, or get the table set. And when the party's over, commandeer some help for the cleanup, too.

Enjoy some wine. If you like wine, have a glass once you've had an hors d'oeuvre or two or during your meal. Having food in your system when you drink slows the absorption of alcohol into your bloodstream and helps keep your blood sugar levels steady. A glass or two of either red or white wine is fine. Avoid beer (except for the occasional light beer), high-sugar types of alcohol, such as apertifs and ice wines, and mixed drinks.

Delight in dessert. Special occasions and dessert go hand in hand. If you like sweets, cut yourself a small piece of cake or select a cookie. Savor the dessert slowly, taking breaks between small bites. Or try the "Three-Bite Rule": Take three bites and then put the dessert aside for a few minutes; most likely you won't come back to it. Do this often enough and you'll discover that just a few tastes of a great dessert can be very satisfying.

Love the leftovers. The healthy leftovers you might have after a South Beach Diet party can be a blessing after all that cooking! Wrap extras in single portions to freeze and eat later in the week or wrap and send items home with your guests as a reminder of a great occasion.

Now Think of Your Own Reasons to Celebrate!

As this book shows, life itself offers an endless array of entertaining opportunities. But who really needs a special reason to celebrate when simply bringing friends and family together for a great meal can be reason enough?

Turn to this cookbook again and again as you bring the many festivities of each year into your home. And, as each occasion arrives, savor every moment as you enjoy the healthy choices of your South Beach Diet lifestyle.

Checklist for Success

Entertaining is the most fun when you feel well prepared beforehand and on party day. Keep this checklist handy to use as a guide. You can do as little or as much as you like ahead of time.

Four to Six Weeks Before

☐ Decide what type of party you want to throw and how many people you want to invite.

☐ Make your invitation list.

☐ Send the invitations.

☐ Order special items, such as a fresh turkey for Thanksgiving.

Two to Four Weeks Before

☐ Check with your guests regarding any special food needs or allergies and adjust the menu, if necessary.

☐ Shop for dry pantry ingredients, drinks, paper goods (including special napkins or cocktail napkins and extra paper towels, tissues, and toilet paper), votive and taper candles, balloons, crepe paper, camera batteries, games for the kids, sunscreen, citronella candles, and bug repellant (for outdoor parties).

☐ Buy groceries for make-ahead dishes.

☐ Review party or holiday Game Plan.

☐ Prepare and freeze make-ahead dishes.

☐ Think through any extra items you might need and make arrangements to rent or purchase them or to borrow them from a friend. For example, you might need special pots or pans, baking dishes, a cake stand or cake knife, special table linens, extra chairs, or extra hangers for coats.

☐ Purchase or make theme-oriented items, if desired.

One Week Before

☐ Shop for perishables, as well as fresh coffee, a selection of black and herbal teas, fat-free or reduced-fat milk, fat-free half-and-half, and sugar substitute.

- [ ] Launder and press tablecloths and cloth napkins.
- [ ] Polish silver.
- [ ] Clean the house.
- [ ] Prepare party favors: These are not necessary but can be fun. For example, you could make extra Holiday Spiced Nuts (page 209) and wrap them in cellophane bags tied with colorful ribbon. Or you could give small bottles of flavored or plain extra-virgin olive oil as healthy South Beach Diet parting gifts.

A Few Days Before

- [ ] Decide where coats will go.
- [ ] Set up the dining and buffet tables and chairs.
- [ ] Make notes for any special toasts (or roasts!) you may want to give.
- [ ] Set aside special music to play.

On Party Day

- [ ] Eat a healthy breakfast.
- [ ] Finish preparing the food as early as possible.
- [ ] Have your midmorning snack.
- [ ] Pick up fresh flowers or pick them from your garden, if using.
- [ ] Schedule time to exercise, outdoors if possible, so you can get some fresh air.
- [ ] Stay hydrated.
- [ ] Have your lunch and midafternoon snack.
- [ ] Empty the dishwasher before the party so that dirty dishes can go right in later.
- [ ] Set out and light votive and taper candles.
- [ ] Set out and light citronella candles for outdoor affairs.
- [ ] Enjoy yourself!

PARTIES

PHASE 1 KICKOFF PARTY

FOR 8 GUESTS

Choosing the South Beach Diet is more than cause for celebration. By taking this first step, you are already on your way to a world of delicious, nutrient-rich foods and a lifetime of better health. So round up a group of friends who all want to embark on a healthy lifestyle and throw this great party. By starting the diet together you'll have fun sharing tips and supporting each other throughout.

The recipes here are simple and quick to prepare, but you'll find that it's the variety of great flavors that makes this meal so satisfying. Cool cucumber sticks get even cooler with a Greek-style yogurt dip, and basil-marinated fresh mozzarella sandwiched between juicy cherry tomatoes turns a favorite Italian salad into a new hors d'oeuvre.

And that's just the beginning. By the end of the party, your guests won't believe that all this fabulous food is part of Phase 1, especially when you present the grand finale—a velvety chocolate mousse with golden almonds and toasted coconut.

◄ *Ocean blue serving platters and pretty shells set a South Beach mood for your Phase 1 Kickoff. You can make this menu for lunch or dinner.*

MENU

Cucumber Sticks with Tzatziki Dip

Caprese Skewers

Creamy Broccoli Soup

Grilled Rosemary-Lemon Chicken

Warm Chickpea Salad

Spinach and Radicchio Salad

Cocoa-Nut Mousse

Party Game Plan

Up to 1 month before: Make and freeze soup.

Up to 2 days before: Make tzatziki dip; season mozzarella; make chickpea salad.

Up to 1 day before: Marinate chicken; prepare mousse.

Day of: Cut cucumber sticks; assemble caprese skewers; thaw and heat soup; finish chickpea salad; make spinach salad; grill chicken.

Cucumber Sticks with Tzatziki Dip

PREP TIME: 10 minutes

This refreshing appetizer is inspired by the traditional Greek tzatziki, a sauce made with yogurt, garlic, and cucumber that's used as both a dip and a condiment for meats and fish. Our version leaves the cucumbers on the side for dipping. Use very fresh garlic for best flavor.

2	medium cucumbers
¾	cup nonfat plain yogurt
1½	teaspoons extra-virgin olive oil
1	tablespoon chopped fresh dill
1	small garlic clove, minced
⅛	teaspoon salt
	Freshly ground black pepper

Trim cucumber ends and peel cucumbers lengthwise to make "zebra stripes," alternating peeled and unpeeled sections. Cut cucumbers lengthwise and seed. Cut each half in half crosswise, then cut into 24 (⅛-inch-thick) sticks.

Whisk together yogurt, oil, dill, garlic, and salt in a small bowl; season to taste with pepper. Serve dip chilled or at room temperature with cucumber sticks.

Makes 8 (3-piece) servings and ¾ cup dip

NUTRITION AT A GLANCE
Per serving (with 1½ tablespoons dip): 25 calories, 1 g fat, 0 g saturated fat, 1 g protein, 3 g carbohydrate, 0.5 g fiber, 50 mg sodium

MAKE-AHEAD: Dip can be made up to 2 days in advance; store in a covered container in the refrigerator. If dip separates, whisk well just before serving.

TIP **About garlic:** A green-colored shoot in the center of a clove of garlic indicates that it is old. If you encounter this, discard the clove and start with a fresh one, or remove the shoot with a paring knife before mincing the clove. You can cook with old garlic, but it's best not to use it raw, as the flavor can be very intense.

Caprese Skewers

PREP TIME: 10 minutes

Fresh mozzarella cheese, tomatoes, and basil make a traditional Italian salad, which becomes a wonderful appetizer here. While assembling the toothpick skewers, keep a damp paper towel by your side to wipe your fingers after assembling each one; this will keep each toothpick clean as you go.

3 ounces fresh mozzarella cheese, cut into 24 (¼- to ½-inch) cubes

1½ teaspoons extra-virgin olive oil

¼ teaspoon dried basil or 3 or 4 fresh basil leaves, julienned

Crushed red pepper flakes

Salt and freshly ground black pepper

24 grape tomatoes, cut in half crosswise

Toss mozzarella with oil, basil, and a pinch or two of pepper flakes in a medium bowl. Season to taste with salt and pepper. Add tomatoes and stir gently to coat. Place 2 tomato halves and 1 mozzarella cube on each of 24 toothpicks, with cheese in between tomatoes. Serve at room temperature.

Makes 8 (3-skewer) servings

NUTRITION AT A GLANCE
Per serving: 50 calories, 3.5 g fat, 1.5 g saturated fat, 2 g protein, 2 g carbohydrate, 0 g fiber, 20 mg sodium

MAKE-AHEAD: Mozzarella can be seasoned with oil, basil, and pepper flakes and refrigerated in a covered container for up to 2 days. Before serving, bring to room temperature, then toss with tomatoes, place on toothpicks, and serve. Skewers can be assembled up to 6 hours in advance; place on a pretty platter, cover with plastic wrap, and refrigerate. Bring to room temperature before guests arrive.

TIP **Festive skewers:** Purchase wooden toothpicks with colorful fringes to create a more lively presentation.

Creamy Broccoli Soup

PREP TIME: 10 minutes   **COOK TIME:** 40 minutes

Flavorful and deeply satisfying, this soup has a creamy texture that belies the fact that it doesn't actually contain any cream. Since it is filling and there's a big meal ahead, we've made small portions. Try serving the soup in beautiful shallow bowls or in pretty teacups with small spoons.

1   tablespoon extra-virgin olive oil

1   large onion, finely chopped

2   garlic cloves, minced

2   pounds broccoli, stems and crowns, roughly chopped

¼   teaspoon salt

     Freshly ground black pepper

5   cups vegetable broth

¼   cup fresh lemon juice

     Small blanched broccoli florets for garnish (optional)

Heat oil over medium heat in a large nonstick saucepan. Add onion and garlic, reduce heat to low, and cook until softened, about 7 minutes. Add broccoli, salt, and a pinch of pepper; stir well to coat. Add broth and lemon juice; bring to a simmer. Partially cover, reduce heat to low, and simmer gently until broccoli is very tender, about 25 minutes.

Transfer soup to a blender and purée, in batches if necessary, or use a hand blender. Serve hot, garnished with a small broccoli floret, if desired.

Makes 8 (1-cup) servings

NUTRITION AT A GLANCE
Per serving: 80 calories, 2.5 g fat, 0 g saturated fat, 4 g protein, 12 g carbohydrate, 4 g fiber, 390 mg sodium

MAKE-AHEAD: Soup can be made up to 3 days in advance and refrigerated in a covered container. It can also be frozen for up to 1 month.

Grilled Rosemary-Lemon Chicken

PREP TIME: 10 minutes   **MARINATING TIME:** 1 hour or overnight   **COOK TIME:** 10 minutes

Marinating the chicken before cooking enchances the perky citrus and herb flavors of this dish. Grilling adds flavor, too, and the grill marks make for a beautiful plate.

½ cup extra-virgin olive oil

¼ cup fresh lemon juice

1 tablespoon plus 1 teaspoon fresh rosemary
    or 2 teaspoons dried rosemary

8 (6-ounce) boneless, skinless chicken breasts

¼ teaspoon salt

¼ teaspoon freshly ground black pepper

1 lemon, cut into 8 wedges

Place oil, lemon juice, and rosemary in a blender or food processor and process until rosemary is coarsely chopped, about 1 minute. Place chicken in a shallow baking dish and pour rosemary mixture over chicken; turn to coat. Sprinkle breasts evenly with salt and pepper. Cover with plastic wrap and marinate 1 hour at room temperature or in the refrigerator overnight.

Heat a grill or grill pan to medium-high. Remove chicken from marinade and grill until cooked through, 4 to 5 minutes per side. Discard leftover marinade. Serve warm or at room temperature with lemon wedges.

Makes 8 (6-ounce) servings

NUTRITION AT A GLANCE
Per serving: 250 calories, 9 g fat, 1.5 g saturated fat, 39 g protein, 1 g carbohydrate, 0 g fiber, 180 mg sodium

MAKE-AHEAD: Chicken can be marinated up to 1 day in advance and can be grilled up to 6 hours before guests arrive. Once grilled, cover and refrigerate, then bring to room temperature or warm gently before serving.

Warm Chickpea Salad

PREP TIME: 10 minutes   **COOK TIME:** 20 minutes

This tasty warm side dish is a perfect match for chicken and also pairs well with sturdy fresh fish, such as tuna or bass, or with steak. With the addition of a few cooked vegetables, such as cauliflower, mustard greens, or mushrooms, this would also make a terrific vegetarian main course.

¼	cup extra-virgin olive oil
1	medium onion, roughly chopped
4	garlic cloves, thinly sliced
½	teaspoon dried thyme
3	(15-ounce) cans chickpeas, rinsed and drained
1½	tablespoons red wine vinegar
3	celery stalks with leaves, finely chopped
	Salt and freshly ground black pepper
	Whole celery leaves (optional)

Heat oil in a medium saucepan over medium heat. Add onion, garlic, and thyme; reduce heat to medium-low and cook, stirring occasionally to ensure that vegetables do not brown, until well softened, about 10 minutes.

Add chickpeas and vinegar; stir to coat. Cover and cook until chickpeas are warmed through, about 5 minutes. Stir in chopped celery. Season to taste with salt and pepper and garnish with celery leaves, if using. Serve warm.

Makes 12 (½-cup) servings

NUTRITION AT A GLANCE

Per serving: 140 calories, 6 g fat, 0.5 g saturated fat, 4 g protein, 20 g carbohydrate, 4 g fiber, 250 mg sodium

MAKE-AHEAD: Salad can be prepared up to 2 days in advance, through the warming of the chickpeas. Refrigerate in a covered container, then rewarm gently on the stove top or in a microwave, adding celery and garnishing with celery leaves, if using, just before serving.

Spinach and Radicchio Salad

PREP TIME: 5 minutes

This salad's citrusy dressing echoes the flavors in the chicken dish and provides a perfect complement to the warm chickpea salad.

6 ounces baby spinach (8 cups)

1 medium (½-pound) head radicchio, cored and cut into ¼-inch slices (4 cups)

3 tablespoons extra-virgin olive oil

1 tablespoon fresh lemon juice

Salt and freshly ground black pepper

Combine spinach and radicchio in a large bowl.

Whisk together oil and lemon juice in a small bowl; add salt and pepper to taste, and whisk again. Pour dressing over salad, toss, and serve.

Makes 8 (1½-cup) servings

NUTRITION AT A GLANCE

Per serving: 70 calories, 5 g fat, 0.5 g saturated fat, 1 g protein, 5 g carbohydrate, 2 g fiber, 60 mg sodium

MAKE-AHEAD: Greens can be rinsed and dried up to 8 hours before serving. Loosely wrap in paper towels, place in a large resealable plastic bag with the air pressed out, and refrigerate until ready to use.

TIP

Buying and storing radicchio: Radicchio is available year-round in most supermarkets; look for firm heads with bright, unblemished leaves. Wrapped in paper towels and stored in an airtight plastic bag in the refrigerator, radicchio should last for up to a week.

Cocoa-Nut Mousse

PREP TIME: 20 minutes   **COOK TIME:** 20 minutes   **CHILL TIME:** 2 hours or overnight

Toasted coconut, cocoa, and almonds—a familiar (and favorite!) candy bar combination—come together in this creamy, decadent mousse. And as if that isn't good enough, the nuts and ricotta cheese offer a dose of healthy protein, making a dessert that is both filling and satisfying to your sweet tooth. What an inspiring way to kick off your South Beach Diet lifestyle!

½ cup slivered almonds

¼ cup shredded unsweetened coconut

4 cups part-skim ricotta cheese

3 tablespoons unsweetened cocoa powder

1 tablespoon plus 1 teaspoon granular sugar substitute

2 teaspoons almond extract

2 teaspoons vanilla extract

1 cup light or fat-free whipped topping

A few slivered almonds and a pinch of coconut for garnish (optional)

Heat oven to 275°F. Spread almonds on a baking sheet and toast until golden and fragrant, stirring occasionally, 8 to 10 minutes. Transfer to a plate to cool. Spread coconut on the baking sheet and toast until golden, 2 to 3 minutes. Transfer to a plate to cool.

In a large bowl, beat ricotta with an electric mixer at high speed until light and airy, about 4 minutes. Add cocoa powder, sugar substitute, and almond and vanilla extracts; beat just until blended. Fold in whipped topping, almonds, and coconut.

Spoon mousse into 8 dessert cups; cover and chill at least 2 hours. To serve, remove mousse from refrigerator and sprinkle lightly with a few almonds and a little coconut, if desired.

Makes 8 (⅔-cup) servings

NUTRITION AT A GLANCE
Per serving: 260 calories, 16 g fat, 8 g saturated fat, 16 g protein, 12 g carbohydrate, 2 g fiber, 160 mg sodium

MAKE-AHEAD: Mousse can be prepared up to 1 day in advance; chill in dessert cups, covered with plastic wrap, until ready to serve. Top with almonds and coconut, if using, just before serving.

FAMILY BUFFET

FOR 10 GUESTS

Alively family gathering filled with lots of chatter, good games, and great food is always a pleasure. Thrown buffet-style, it's all the merrier. Once the meal is set out, there's hardly a fuss to be had in the kitchen, leaving you with time to catch up with everyone.

Host this party indoors or out—anything goes! A starter of lean grilled beef hot dogs, cut into playful bite-size pieces and served with three tasty dipping sauces, is just as at home by the fire on a chilly day as it is under the sun in good kickball company. Asparagus spears are dressed up with thin, lean slices of ham and drizzled with healthy extra-virgin olive oil. Our crisp, nutty Waldorf salad proves that even the great classics can get an easy, healthy makeover and leaves room for baked chicken and a yummy pasta dish. And family members of all ages will love the fabulous fruit pops for dessert.

◀ *This party for 10 offers plenty of food for young and old alike. The hot dogs and pasta will especially appeal to the kids.*

MENU

Dogs 'n' Dips

Asparagus and Ham Spears

Baked Chicken with Artichokes

South Beach Waldorf Salad

Penne with Homemade Tomato Sauce

Banana-Orange Pops

Party Game Plan

Up to 1 month before: Make and freeze pasta sauce.

Up to 5 days before: Make and freeze banana pops.

Up to 2 days before: Boil pasta.

Up to 1 day before: Prepare asparagus; make mustard dip; prepare chicken; thaw pasta sauce.

Day of: Assemble asparagus spears; make red pepper dip and sauerkraut dip; bake chicken; prepare salad; grill hot dogs; finish penne and sauce.

Dogs 'n' Dips

Loved by kids of all ages, hot dogs are no strangers to family feasts. Here's a new spin on serving them that will appeal to the whole gang. Have decorative toothpicks on hand for skewering the dogs and little serving bowls for the dips. Lean beef dogs can be replaced by turkey or vegetarian hot dogs, if desired.

Dogs

PREP TIME: 5 minutes   **COOK TIME:** 10 minutes

    5 (97% fat-free) beef hot dogs

Heat a grill pan over medium-high heat. Grill hot dogs until well browned on all sides, 7 to 10 minutes. Remove from pan, allow to cool slightly, and slice each hot dog on the bias into 8 equal pieces (about ¾ inch each). Skewer each piece with a toothpick and set on a serving platter. Serve warm with dips.

Makes 10 (4-piece) servings

NUTRITION AT A GLANCE
Per serving: 25 calories, 1 g fat, 0 g saturated fat, 3 g protein, 2 g carbohydrate, 0 g fiber, 200 mg sodium

Herbed Mustard Dip

PREP TIME: 5 minutes

½ cup Dijon mustard	½ cup chopped fresh basil
2 tablespoons mayonnaise	1 tablespoon minced red onion

Stir together mustard, mayonnaise, basil, and onion in a small bowl. Serve with hot dogs.

Makes ⅔ cup

NUTRITION AT A GLANCE
Per tablespoon: 20 calories, 2 g fat, 0 g saturated fat, 0 g protein, 0 g carbohydrate, 0 g fiber, 170 mg sodium

MAKE-AHEAD: Dip can be prepared up to 1 day ahead; refrigerate in a covered container and bring to room temperature before serving.

Roasted Red Pepper Dip

PREP TIME: 5 minutes

> 3 large roasted red peppers (from a jar)
>
> 3 tablespoons low-fat (1%) cottage cheese
>
> Freshly ground black pepper
>
> Hot pepper sauce (optional)

Purée red peppers and cottage cheese in a blender or food processor until smooth. Season to taste with black pepper and pepper sauce, if using. Serve with hot dogs.

Makes 1 cup

NUTRITION AT A GLANCE

Per tablespoon: 10 calories, 0 g fat, 0 g saturated fat, 1 g protein, 1 g carbohydrate, 0 g fiber, 65 mg sodium

MAKE-AHEAD: Dip can be made up to 6 hours ahead; refrigerate in a covered container and bring to room temperature before serving.

Sauerkraut Dip

PREP TIME: 5 minutes

> ½ cup sauerkraut, finely chopped
>
> ¼ cup plus 2 tablespoons reduced-fat sour cream
>
> 1 celery stalk, minced
>
> Freshly ground black pepper

Stir together sauerkraut, sour cream, and celery in a small bowl. Season to taste with pepper. Serve with hot dogs.

Makes 1 cup

NUTRITION AT A GLANCE

Per tablespoon: 10 calories, 0.5 g fat, 0 g saturated fat, 0 g protein, 1 g carbohydrate, 0 g fiber, 35 mg sodium

MAKE-AHEAD: Dip can be made up to 6 hours ahead; refrigerate in a covered container and bring to room temperature before serving.

Asparagus and Ham Spears

PREP TIME: 20 minutes   **COOK TIME:** 2 minutes

Asparagus are widely available year-round, making this easy hors d'oeuvre a sure bet for any season. The thinner the ham, the better it will wrap around the asparagus spears. For best results, ask your butcher to slice it to about $\frac{1}{16}$ inch thick.

1¼ pounds medium asparagus, tough ends trimmed

¼ pound thinly sliced lower-fat, lower-sodium smoked ham (not honey glazed)

1 tablespoon plus 1 teaspoon extra-virgin olive oil

1 teaspoon grated lemon zest

Freshly ground black pepper

Bring a large saucepan of lightly salted water to a boil. Add asparagus and cook just until crisp-tender, about 1½ minutes. Drain in a colander and immediately run asparagus under very cold water for 1 minute to stop cooking. Drain again and pat dry.

Cut ham slices lengthwise into ½-inch-wide strips. Wrap ham strips around asparagus spears, beginning right below the tips. Place spears on a serving platter and drizzle with oil. Sprinkle with zest, season with several pinches of pepper, and serve.

Makes 10 servings

NUTRITION AT A GLANCE
Per serving: 50 calories, 3 g fat, 0.5 g saturated fat, 4 g protein, 2 g carbohydrate, 1 g fiber, 110 mg sodium

MAKE-AHEAD: Asparagus can be cooked, drained, and patted dry up to 1 day ahead. Refrigerate in a covered container until ready to use. You can wrap with ham up to 6 hours ahead, cover with plastic wrap, and refrigerate. Bring to room temperature before drizzling with oil; finish with zest and pepper just before serving.

Baked Chicken with Artichokes

PREP TIME: 10 minutes   **COOK TIME:** 40 minutes

This Mediterranean-style chicken makes great buffet fare. Browning the chicken first adds flavor and a great look to the dish, while baking it covered creates very moist results. You'll need two large baking dishes for this recipe.

10	(6-ounce) boneless, skinless chicken breasts
½	teaspoon salt
¼	teaspoon freshly ground black pepper
3	tablespoons extra-virgin olive oil
1	medium red onion, sliced
2	(8-ounce) jars quartered artichokes, drained
1	lemon, cut into 10 slices
1	teaspoon dried oregano
1	teaspoon dried thyme

Heat oven to 350°F. Lightly coat 2 large baking dishes with cooking spray. Season chicken with salt and pepper, and set aside on a large platter.

Heat 1 tablespoon of the oil in a large nonstick skillet over medium high heat. Add onion and cook, stirring occasionally, until softened, about 5 minutes. Divide onion between the baking dishes.

Heat remaining 2 tablespoons oil in the same skillet over medium-high heat. Add chicken, in batches, if necessary, and cook until lightly browned, about 5 minutes per side. Divide chicken between the baking dishes.

Divide artichokes between the dishes, arranging around chicken. Place 1 lemon slice on top of each chicken breast. Sprinkle breasts evenly with oregano and thyme.

Cover baking dishes with foil and bake 10 to 15 minutes, or until artichokes are heated through. Serve warm.

Makes 10 (6-ounce) servings

NUTRITION AT A GLANCE
Per serving: 260 calories, 8 g fat, 1 g saturated fat, 40 g protein, 5 g carbohydrate, 1 g fiber, 330 mg sodium

MAKE-AHEAD: This dish can be prepared up to the point of baking 1 day in advance. Cover and refrigerate, then bake as directed (baking time may take longer).

South Beach Waldorf Salad

PREP TIME: 15 minutes   **COOK TIME:** 10 minutes

New York's great Waldorf-Astoria Hotel in the late 19th century was the birthplace of this now well-known salad, especially beloved for its combination of crunchy apple, crisp celery, creamy mayo, and toasted walnuts. Here we have added reduced-fat sour cream to lighten up the dressing.

- 1 cup walnut pieces
- 1 (¾-pound) head romaine lettuce, cut into bite-size pieces (8 to 10 cups)
- 2 small Granny Smith apples, diced
- 4 celery stalks, diced
- 2 tablespoons mayonnaise
- 2 tablespoons reduced-fat sour cream
- 1 tablespoon plus 1 teaspoon fresh lemon juice
- ¼ teaspoon salt

  Freshly ground black pepper

Heat oven to 275°F. Place walnuts on a baking sheet and toast until lightly browned, about 10 minutes. Cool briefly and chop.

Toss lettuce, apples, celery, and walnuts together in a large serving bowl.

Whisk together mayonnaise, sour cream, lemon juice, and salt in a small bowl. Pour dressing over lettuce mixture and toss to coat. Season to taste with pepper and serve.

Makes 10 (2-cup) servings

NUTRITION AT A GLANCE

Per serving: 130 calories, 10 g fat, 1.5 g saturated fat, 3 g protein, 8 g carbohydrate, 2 g fiber, 100 mg sodium

MAKE-AHEAD: Dressing can be made up to 6 hours ahead; refrigerate in a covered container and whisk before adding to salad.

Penne with Homemade Tomato Sauce

PREP TIME: 10 minutes   **COOK TIME:** 35 minutes

This tasty pasta dish is meant as a side dish for the chicken. The kids will love it, so if you're expecting lots of youngsters, make extra.

2 tablespoons extra-virgin olive oil	3 (14.5-ounce) cans unsalted diced tomatoes
1 medium onion, finely chopped	½ teaspoon salt
3 garlic cloves, minced	Freshly ground black pepper
2 teaspoons dried basil	1 (16-ounce) package whole-wheat penne pasta
¼ teaspoon crushed red pepper flakes	

Bring a large pot of lightly salted water to a boil.

Heat oil in a large nonstick saucepan over medium heat. Add onion, garlic, basil, and pepper flakes. Reduce heat to medium-low and cook, stirring frequently, until onions and garlic are softened, 5 to 7 minutes.

Add tomatoes and salt and bring sauce to a simmer. Reduce heat to low and simmer gently, stirring occasionally, for 20 minutes. Season with pepper to taste.

While sauce is cooking, add pasta to boiling water and cook to al dente, according to package directions. Drain, toss with tomato sauce, and serve hot.

Makes 10 (1-cup) servings

NUTRITION AT A GLANCE
Per serving: 230 calories, 4 g fat, 0 g saturated fat, 7 g protein, 41 g carbohydrate, 6 g fiber, 170 mg sodium

MAKE-AHEAD: Sauce can be made up to 3 days in advance and refrigerated in a covered container. Or it can be frozen up to 1 month ahead. Pasta can be made up to 2 days ahead; drain, run under cold water, and store in a covered container in the refrigerator. When ready to use, combine pasta and sauce in a baking dish and gently reheat, covered, in a 325°F oven.

TIP **To peel garlic easily:** Place a clove on a cutting board. Trim the bottom and discard, then gently smash the clove with the flat side of a chef's knife. The peel will crack and should easily come apart from the clove.

Banana-Orange Pops

PREP TIME: 10 minutes   **FREEZING TIME:** 4 hours or overnight

These sherbet-like frozen treats make a refreshing end to a family meal and are sure to please kids, both young and old. You'll need 10 (3-ounce) paper cups and 10 wooden sticks.

> 2 ripe bananas
>
> ¼ cup undiluted orange juice concentrate, thawed
>
> 1 cup nonfat or low-fat plain yogurt

Purée bananas, orange juice concentrate, and yogurt in a food processor or blender until smooth.

Divide mixture evenly among paper cups. Insert a wooden stick into the center of each pop. Freeze until pops are frozen, at least 4 hours or overnight. When ready to serve, peel off paper cups.

Makes 10 pops

NUTRITION AT A GLANCE

Per pop: 70 calories, 0.5 g fat, 0 g saturated fat, 3 g protein, 13 g carbohydrate, 0 g fiber, 40 mg sodium

MAKE-AHEAD: Pops can be made 5 days ahead. Leave in paper cups and store in a resealable freezer-proof plastic bag; remove cups before serving.

BABY SHOWER

FOR 10 GUESTS

Everyone loves celebrating a mom-to-be. Not only is a baby shower one of the best ways to express our happiness and excitement for a friend or family member, it's also a fun-filled party where food that's both elegant and nutritious really makes the day.

Have your guests start by nibbling on assorted raw veggies with arugula pesto dip or herb and citrus cream cheese on cucumber wheels. After they mingle and chat, invite them back to the buffet to enjoy elegant turkey and watercress tea sandwiches, rosemary-scented shrimp, and two beautiful salads. These crowd-pleasing dishes provide plenty of lean protein and a host of vitamins and minerals.

When you bring out dessert, your guest of honor will be more than thrilled. The lovely stacked cakes, with frosting in pink or blue or both, will show her just how much thought and planning you put into her special day.

◄ *Serving this luncheon buffet-style allows guests to help themselves and then enjoy the food while the guest of honor opens her presents.*

MENU

Crudités with Arugula Pesto Dip

Herb and Citrus Cream Cheese on Cucumber Wheels

Turkey and Watercress Tea Sandwiches

Grilled Shrimp on Rosemary "Skewers"

White Bean and Spinach Salad

Chopped Salad with Dijon Vinaigrette

Boy or Girl Angel Cakes

Party Game Plan

Up to 1 month before: Make and freeze cake.

Up to 2 days before: Prepare cheese for cucumbers; thaw cake.

Up to 1 day before: Make pesto dip and sandwich spread; marinate shrimp; prepare chopped salad vegetables (except lettuce); prepare vinaigrettes for both salads.

Day of: Cut crudités; make cake filling; assemble cucumber wheels, sandwiches, salads, and cakes; grill shrimp skewers.

Crudités with Arugula Pesto Dip

PREP TIME: 30 minutes (with crudités)   **CHILL TIME:** 1 hour or overnight

Leafy arugula lends pleasant earth tones and a peppery flavor to this fun dip, but that's not all. The green also contributes plenty of nutrients including folate, fiber, and calcium.

- 2 large bunches basil, leaves picked and stems discarded
- 1 large bunch arugula, trimmed
- ¼ cup pine nuts
- 1 medium garlic clove, peeled
- ½ teaspoon salt
- 6 tablespoons extra-virgin olive oil
- 2 tablespoons fresh lemon juice
- 2 tablespoons reduced-fat sour cream

    Assorted fresh vegetables, such as asparagus, bell peppers, carrots, endive, radishes, and snow peas, cut up for dipping

Finely grind basil, arugula, pine nuts, garlic, and salt in a food processor or blender.

With machine running, add oil and lemon juice in a slow and steady stream. Add sour cream and process briefly just to combine. Transfer to a serving bowl, cover, and chill for 1 hour or overnight for flavors to blend. Serve at room temperature with assorted vegetables for dipping.

Makes 1½ cups dip

NUTRITION AT A GLANCE
Per tablespoon: 45 calories, 4.5 g fat, 0.5 g saturated fat, 0 g protein, 1 g carbohydrate, 0 g fiber, 50 mg sodium

MAKE-AHEAD: Dip can be made up to 1 day in advance and refrigerated in a covered container. Bring to room temperature before serving.

Herb and Citrus Cream Cheese on Cucumber Wheels

PREP TIME: 20 minutes

This lemony cheese spread, flavored with fresh herbs and red onion, offers something new atop a cucumber slice.

4 ounces reduced-fat cream cheese, at room temperature

3 tablespoons chopped fresh basil

2 tablespoons chopped fresh parsley

2 teaspoons minced red onion

1 teaspoon finely grated lemon zest

1 teaspoon fresh lemon juice

⅛ teaspoon freshly ground black pepper

1 large (8-inch-long) cucumber or 2 smaller cucumbers

Whisk together cream cheese, basil, parsley, onion, zest, lemon juice, and pepper in a medium bowl.

Trim cucumber ends and peel cucumber lengthwise to make "zebra stripes," alternating peeled and unpeeled sections. Slice into 30 (¼-inch-thick) rounds.

Top each cucumber round with a heaping ½ teaspoon cheese mixture. Transfer to a platter and serve.

Makes 10 (3-piece) servings

NUTRITION AT A GLANCE
Per serving: 30 calories, 1.5 g fat, 1 g saturated fat, 1 g protein, 2 g carbohydrate, 0 g fiber, 35 mg sodium

MAKE-AHEAD: Cheese mixture can be made up to 2 days in advance and refrigerated in a covered container. Bring to room temperature before spreading onto cucumber wheels.

Turkey and Watercress Tea Sandwiches

PREP TIME: 15 minutes

Tea sandwiches are enjoying something of a renaissance, and they should: Easy to prepare and easy to eat, they make great party fare. These are dressed up with a homemade spread that makes them eminently worthy of this very special occasion. Be sure to use oven-roasted turkey, not smoked; it's better for the pregnant mom.

¼ cup mayonnaise

¼ cup reduced-fat sour cream

1 tablespoon chopped fresh basil

1 teaspoon chopped fresh chives

1 teaspoon fresh lemon juice

Freshly ground black pepper

10 thin slices whole-grain bread

5 ounces thinly sliced oven-roasted turkey

1 bunch watercress, thick stems removed

Whisk together mayonnaise, sour cream, basil, chives, lemon juice, and a pinch of pepper in a small bowl.

Spread mayonnaise mixture evenly on 5 slices of the bread (you can remove the crusts if you like). Place turkey slices and watercress evenly on top, then top with remaining bread. Cut sandwiches into quarters and serve.

Makes 10 (2-piece) servings

NUTRITION AT A GLANCE

Per serving: 120 calories, 6 g fat, 1 g saturated fat, 5 g protein, 11 g carbohydrate, 1 g fiber, 300 mg sodium

MAKE-AHEAD: Spread can be made up to 1 day ahead and refrigerated in a covered container until ready to use. Sandwiches can be made up to 4 hours before the party; keep them well wrapped and refrigerated; allow to come to room temperature, cut into quarters, and serve.

Grilled Shrimp on Rosemary "Skewers"

PREP TIME: 10 minutes **MARINATING TIME:** 1 hour or overnight **COOK TIME:** 10 minutes

Rosemary skewers are easy to make and very beautiful when set out on a pretty serving platter. Look for herb branches with thick, woody stems—these will hold up through the grilling process. Use extra lemon wedges as a garnish, if you like.

- 3 tablespoons extra-virgin olive oil
- 2 garlic cloves, minced
- 1 tablespoon fresh lemon juice
- 1 teaspoon finely grated lemon zest
- ¼ teaspoon freshly ground black pepper
- 3 tablespoons chopped fresh rosemary
- 30 jumbo shrimp, peeled and deveined
- 10 rosemary sprigs, at least 8 inches long, with thick, woody stems
- Salt

Whisk together oil, garlic, lemon juice, zest, pepper, and chopped rosemary in a medium bowl. Add shrimp and toss to coat; cover and refrigerate for at least 1 hour or overnight.

Wrap 3 marinated shrimp around each rosemary sprig, leaving at least ¼ inch between shrimp for even cooking. Season lightly with salt. Heat a grill or grill pan to medium-high. Grill shrimp, brushing with any leftover marinade, until cooked through, 3 to 4 minutes per side. Discard any remaining marinade. Transfer shrimp on skewers onto a serving platter and serve warm or at room temperature.

Makes 10 servings

NUTRITION AT A GLANCE
Per serving: 60 calories, 4.5 g fat, 0.5 g saturated fat, 4 g protein, 1 g carbohydrate, 0 g fiber, 30 mg sodium

MAKE-AHEAD: Shrimp can be marinated 1 hour in advance or overnight in the refrigerator in a resealable plastic bag.

White Bean and Spinach Salad

PREP TIME: 35 minutes   **COOK TIME:** 2 minutes

Remarkably easy, this bean salad is also stunning and very tasty. Slice the red onion as thinly as possible; when you soak it in warm olive oil and lemon juice, the bite will mellow, leaving you with a delightfully sweet and flavorful red onion vinaigrette.

 1 small red onion, very thinly sliced

 3 garlic cloves, minced

 6 tablespoons fresh lemon juice

 ½ teaspoon salt

 ¼ cup extra-virgin olive oil

 3 (15-ounce) cans cannellini beans, rinsed and drained

 1½ cups packed baby spinach (2 ounces)

 Freshly ground black pepper

Combine onion, garlic, lemon juice, and salt in a large serving bowl; stir well.

Heat oil in a small skillet over medium high heat until just warm, about 2 minutes. Slowly and carefully pour warm oil over onion mixture (it will sizzle a bit). Stir well to combine and let sit at room temperature for 20 minutes, stirring occasionally.

Add beans and spinach to the vinaigrette, and toss well to coat. Season with pepper to taste and serve.

Makes 10 servings

NUTRITION AT A GLANCE
Per serving: 130 calories, 6 g fat, 1 g saturated fat, 4 g protein, 15 g carbohydrate, 4 g fiber, 320 mg sodium

MAKE-AHEAD: Vinaigrette can be made up to 1 day ahead and refrigerated in a covered container. Bring to room temperature before tossing with beans and spinach.

Chopped Salad with Dijon Vinaigrette

PREP TIME: 30 minutes

This gorgeous salad bursts with color, texture, and flavor, as every forkful brings up a different combination of lettuce and veggies. Get ready to chop!

- 3 tablespoons red wine vinegar
- 1 tablespoon Dijon mustard
- 2 tablespoons minced red onion
- 1 garlic clove, minced
- Salt and freshly ground black pepper
- ⅓ cup extra-virgin olive oil
- 1 (½-pound) head red leaf lettuce or chicory, chopped (about 4 cups)
- 2 medium fennel bulbs, finely chopped
- 3 yellow bell peppers, finely chopped
- 12 large white mushrooms, stemmed and sliced
- 1 large bunch radishes, cut into thin wedges

Whisk together vinegar, mustard, onion, garlic, and a pinch of salt and pepper in a small bowl. Add oil in a slow and steady stream, whisking to combine.

Make a bed of chopped lettuce on a large platter. Arrange fennel, bell peppers, mushrooms, and radishes decoratively in alternating rows or concentric circles on top of lettuce. Drizzle with dressing and serve.

Makes 10 (generous ½-cup) servings

NUTRITION AT A GLANCE

Per serving: 100 calories, 8 g fat, 1 g saturated fat, 2 g protein, 8 g carbohydrate, 2 g fiber, 75 mg sodium

MAKE-AHEAD: All salad vegetables, except lettuce, can be cleaned, dried well, and chopped up to 1 day in advance; refrigerate in separate covered containers until ready to serve. Dressing can be prepared up to 1 day ahead and refrigerated in a covered container; bring to room temperature and whisk before drizzling on salad.

Boy or Girl Angel Cakes

PREP TIME: 30 minutes   **COOK TIME:** 20 minutes

The sweet filling and topping for these adorable individual cakes is tinted blue or pink in honor of the little one on his or her way.

12 large egg whites	¾ cup granulated sugar substitute
1 teaspoon cream of tartar	¾ cup whole-grain pastry flour
¼ teaspoon salt	2 cups fat-free or light whipped topping
1 teaspoon vanilla extract	
½ teaspoon lemon extract	All-natural red and blue food colorings

Heat oven to 350°F. Coat 2 (8- by 8-inch) glass baking dishes with cooking spray. In a large bowl, beat egg whites, cream of tartar, and salt with electric mixer at high speed until soft peaks form. Add extracts and beat briefly to combine. Gradually add sugar substitute; continue beating whites until stiff peaks form.

Sift ¼ cup of the flour over egg whites. Using a rubber spatula, gently fold in flour until fully combined. Repeat twice with remaining flour until all of the flour is incorporated.

Divide batter evenly between baking dishes, gently smoothing out tops. Bake, turning once halfway through, until cakes are golden and a tester inserted in the center comes out clean, 18 to 20 minutes. Cool completely.

When cakes are cool, cut each into 4 squares and carefully transfer to a cutting board. Trim browned edges, then cut each square into 4 (2-inch) squares. You should have 32 squares total.

Place 1 cup whipped topping in each of 2 small bowls. Add a few drops of red food coloring to 1 bowl and mix. Add a few drops of blue food coloring to the other bowl and mix, if you're making both colors.

Lay squares of cake on a flat work surface, top each with 1½ teaspoons pink or blue topping, spreading filling to just shy of cake edges. Top each with a second cake square and 1½ teaspoons topping.

Makes 16 servings

NUTRITION AT A GLANCE
Per serving: 50 calories, 0 g fat, 0 g saturated fat, 3 g protein, 8 g carbohydrate, 0 g fiber, 85 mg sodium

MAKE-AHEAD: Cake can be made up to 1 month in advance and frozen.

WEEKEND BRUNCH

FOR 8 GUESTS

The scent of nutty, orange scones will fill the kitchen as your guests arrive at this simple weekend gathering. Greet them with a steaming mug of coffee or a hot pot of tea and they'll think they're still dreaming!

Brunch should be a stress-free affair. That's why we've made this menu extra easy and quick to shop for and prepare. The scones can be baked ahead and frozen, then thawed and warmed as guests arrive. You'll cook the eggs casserole-style, giving you time to set the table as they bake. The asparagus require just 15 minutes to roast, and creamy berry smoothies whip up in minutes. Put the dishes out as a buffet, pass them around the table family-style, or make individual plates for each guest, if you prefer. A great party to host for any sort of informal occasion, a weekend brunch can enhance a housewarming, enliven a neighborhood or book-club meeting, or simply be an excuse to introduce old friends to new.

◀ *The dishes at this festive brunch are equally satisfying and nutritious. The rich smoothies serve as both a drink and dessert.*

MENU

Baked Eggs with Spinach and Ham

Roasted Asparagus

Orange-Pecan Scones

Zesty Salad Niçoise

Blueberry-Melon Smoothies

Party Game Plan

Up to 1 month before: Make and freeze scones.

Up to 2 days before: Hard-boil eggs; make salad dressing.

Up to 1 day before: Cut up ham and spinach; blanch green beans.

Day of: Assemble salad; thaw and heat scones; assemble and bake eggs, spinach, and ham; roast asparagus; make smoothies.

Baked Eggs with Spinach and Ham

PREP TIME: 10 minutes   **COOK TIME:** 45 minutes

Eggs baked in a casserole make a classic late-morning dish that's easy to prepare. This one gets added flavor and nutrients, including vitamin B$_6$, folate, and potassium, from baby spinach and onions.

2	tablespoons extra-virgin olive oil
1	small onion, thinly sliced
4	(1-ounce) slices lower-fat, lower-sodium boiled or smoked ham (not honey glazed), cut into thin strips
4	ounces baby spinach, chopped (4 to 5 cups)
12	large eggs
¼	teaspoon salt
⅛	teaspoon freshly ground black pepper

Heat oven to 350°F. Lightly coat an 8- by 8-inch glass baking dish with cooking spray.

Heat 1 tablespoon of the oil in a large nonstick skillet over medium-high heat. Add onion and cook, stirring occasionally, until softened, about 5 minutes. Add ham and cook 3 minutes more. Transfer to a large bowl.

Add remaining 1 tablespoon oil to the pan. Add spinach and cook, stirring occasionally, until spinach is wilted, about 3 minutes. Add to the bowl with the ham and onion mixture.

Whisk together eggs, salt, and pepper in a medium bowl. Pour half of the egg mixture into the baking dish. Scatter onion, ham, and spinach mixture on top of eggs. Cover with remaining egg mixture. Bake until eggs are set and lightly browned, about 30 minutes. Allow to cool for 10 minutes. Cut into squares and serve warm.

Makes 8 servings

NUTRITION AT A GLANCE
Per serving: 170 calories, 12 g fat, 3 g saturated fat, 13 g protein, 3 g carbohydrate, 0 g fiber, 340 mg sodium

MAKE-AHEAD: Ham and spinach can be prepared 1 day ahead and stored in separate covered containers in the refrigerator until ready to use.

Roasted Asparagus

PREP TIME: 5 minutes   **COOK TIME:** 15 minutes

Brightly colored and zesty flavored, these roasted asparagus spears are great on their own, chopped into salads or rice dishes, or served alongside meat or fish. Place a set of pretty tongs out with them for easy serving.

 2 pounds medium asparagus, tough ends trimmed

 2 tablespoons extra-virgin olive oil

 2 teaspoons grated lemon zest

 ¼ teaspoon salt

 ⅛ teaspoon freshly ground black pepper

 1 lemon, cut into 8 wedges

Heat oven to 475°F.

Lay asparagus in a single layer in a large baking pan (you may need to use 2 pans). Drizzle with oil and sprinkle with zest, salt, and pepper. Roll asparagus around pan to coat with oil and seasonings.

Roast until asparagus begins to brown and is easily pierced with a paring knife, 10 to 15 minutes. Serve warm with lemon wedges.

Makes 8 servings

NUTRITION AT A GLANCE
Per serving: 60 calories, 3.5 g fat, 0.5 g saturated fat, 2 g protein, 5 g carbohydrate, 3 g fiber, 75 mg sodium

MAKE-AHEAD: Roasted asparagus can be made up to 6 hours ahead, covered lightly, and kept at room temperature. Serve at room temperature or reheat for a few minutes in a 325°F oven.

Orange-Pecan Scones

PREP TIME: 15 minutes   **COOK TIME:** 25 minutes

The addition of buttermilk helps produce a flaky and flavorful scone. Trans-fat-free margarine softens very quickly, so keep it chilled until you're ready to add it.

⅓ cup pecan pieces

¼ cup 1% or fat-free buttermilk

1 large egg

½ teaspoon vanilla extract

½ teaspoon finely grated orange zest

⅛ teaspoon orange extract

½ cup whole-grain pastry flour

½ cup unbleached all-purpose flour

2 tablespoons granular sugar substitute

2 teaspoons baking powder

½ teaspoon ground cinnamon

¼ teaspoon baking soda

¼ teaspoon salt

½ cup chilled trans-fat-free margarine, cut into bits

Position rack in middle of oven and heat oven to 400°F. Place pecans on a baking sheet and toast until fragrant and lightly golden, 3 to 4 minutes. Remove from oven and cool. Lightly coat a baking sheet with cooking spray.

Whisk together buttermilk, egg, vanilla, zest, and orange extract in a small bowl.

In a large bowl, sift together whole-grain and all-purpose flours, sugar substitute, baking powder, cinnamon, baking soda, and salt. Add margarine and, using a pastry blender or 2 knives, cut margarine into the dry ingredients until the mixture resembles coarse meal. Add pecans and buttermilk mixture, stirring until mixture forms a slightly sticky dough. Using wet hands, knead dough 4 or 5 times in the bowl.

Place dough onto baking sheet and form into a ¾-inch-thick disk. Cut disk all the way through into 8 wedges (do not separate). Bake until lightly golden, 15 to 18 minutes. Serve warm or at room temperature.

Makes 8 scones

NUTRITION AT A GLANCE

Per scone: 190 calories, 14 g fat, 3.5 g saturated fat, 3 g protein, 13 g carbohydrate, 2 g fiber, 270 mg sodium

MAKE-AHEAD: Scones are best eaten shortly after baking, but you can freeze them for up to 1 month in advance. Defrost at room temperature and reheat in a warm oven.

Zesty Salad Niçoise

PREP TIME: 20 minutes   **COOK TIME:** 5 minutes

A variety of textures and flavors makes this salad crisp, refreshing, and very satisfying. Use niçoise olives to add authenticity to the dish.

Dressing

- ⅓ cup extra-virgin olive oil
- 3 tablespoons fresh lemon juice
- 1½ teaspoons Dijon mustard
- 2 teaspoons grated lemon zest
- 1 small garlic clove, minced
- ¼ teaspoon salt
- ⅛ teaspoon freshly ground black pepper
- 24 pitted black olives, finely chopped (½ cup)

Salad

- ½ pound green beans, trimmed
- 3 (6-ounce) cans water-packed chunk light tuna, drained and flaked
- 1 (¾-pound) head romaine lettuce, cut into bite-size pieces
- ¼ teaspoon salt
- ⅛ teaspoon freshly ground black pepper
- 2 medium tomatoes, cut into 8 wedges each
- 2 hard-boiled eggs, finely chopped

For the dressing: Whisk together oil, lemon juice, and mustard in a small bowl. Add zest, garlic, salt, pepper, and olives and whisk to combine.

For the salad: Bring a large saucepan of lightly salted water to a boil. Add beans and cook just until crisp-tender, 2 to 3 minutes. Drain in a colander and immediately run under cold water for 1 minute to stop cooking. Drain again and pat dry. Cut beans into 1-inch pieces.

Mix tuna with ¼ cup of the dressing in a medium bowl. In a large bowl, toss beans, lettuce, salt, and pepper with remaining dressing. Transfer to a serving platter. Spoon tuna mixture onto the center of the greens. Arrange tomato wedges around tuna, sprinkle with chopped egg, and serve.

Makes 8 (2-cup) servings

NUTRITION AT A GLANCE

Per serving: 220 calories, 12 g fat, 2 g saturated fat, 20 g protein, 7 g carbohydrate, 3 g fiber, 390 mg sodium

MAKE-AHEAD: Eggs and dressing can be made up to 2 days in advance and stored in an airtight container in the refrigerator. Green beans can be cooked up to 1 day in advance; pat dry, wrap well in a paper towel, and store in a resealable plastic bag in the refrigerator.

Blueberry-Melon Smoothies

PREP TIME: 10 minutes

The flavors of blueberry and cantaloupe complement each other wonderfully in this colorful dessert-in-a-glass.

1 (3-pound) cantaloupe, seeded and cubed (3 cups)

3 cups frozen blueberries

3 cups nonfat or low-fat sugar-free vanilla yogurt

Ice cubes

Purée 1½ cups of the cantaloupe and 1½ cups of the blueberries in a blender until just combined, about 1 minute. Add 1½ cups of the yogurt and several ice cubes and blend until ice cubes are processed, 1 to 2 minutes. Pour smoothie into 4 glasses. Repeat with remaining ingredients.

Makes 8 (1-cup) drinks

NUTRITION AT A GLANCE
Per drink: 90 calories, 0.5 g fat, 0 g saturated fat, 4 g protein, 20 g carbohydrate, 2 g fiber, 60 mg sodium

TIP **Choosing and storing a melon:** To choose a nice ripe melon, look for one that yields slightly when pressed at the blossom end and smells sweet and perfumy. Once cut, leaving the seeds in a halved melon that's wrapped well and refrigerated will keep it fresh.

SUPER BOWL BASH

FOR 8 GUESTS

At once rowdy and relaxing, Super Bowl Sunday is all about having fun. Whether your guests are big football fans or just enjoy listening to the roar of dueling rivals from afar, everyone will get into the spirited festivities one way or another.

Never "tackled" a gathering like this before? No problem! We show you how simple it is to put South Beach Diet–friendly twists on classic game-watching fare. Start the first half off with two nutritious dips served with veggies and pita triangles, then bring out a platter of fiery Buffalo chicken morsels with light and creamy blue cheese sauce. For the rest of this sporting meal, set out a big pot of tender pork-and-bean chili, a bowl piled high with crisp Caesar salad, and a plate of freshly baked healthy cookies.

You'll want to serve this meal buffet-style, not too far from the TV. This way, you can relax on the sidelines, and your football fans can enjoy the eats without missing a moment of the action!

◄ *As this menu proves, Super Bowl fare doesn't have to be high in fat. Presenting a huge platter of crudités with hummus and eggplant dip is a great way to begin.*

MENU

Sun-Dried Tomato Hummus

Garlicky Eggplant Dip

Buffalo Chicken Bites

Blue Cheese Dipping Sauce

Pork and Poblano Chili

Eggless Tex-Mex Caesar Salad

Ranger Cookies

Party Game Plan

Up to 3 days before: Prepare hummus; make chili.

Up to 1 day before: Prepare blue cheese dip; toast pita chips; make salad dressing; make cookies.

Day of: Prepare eggplant dip; cut crudités; make chicken bites; assemble salad; reheat chili.

Sun-Dried Tomato Hummus

PREP TIME: 10 minutes   **COOK TIME:** 12 minutes

Yogurt and sesame oil replace tahini in this hummus, creating a lighter texture than the norm. If you are on Phase 1, enjoy the green veggies, cauliflower, cherry tomatoes, and bell peppers, and simply skip the carrots and pita chips.

8	(6-inch) whole-wheat pitas, cut into 4 triangles each
1½	cups canned chickpeas, rinsed and drained
¾	cup canned cannellini beans, rinsed and drained
4	sun-dried tomatoes (packed in oil), plus 1 tablespoon of the oil
1	small garlic clove, peeled
¼	cup nonfat or low-fat plain yogurt
2	tablespoons fresh lemon juice
½	teaspoon toasted sesame oil
¼	teaspoon ground cumin
¼	teaspoon salt
	Assorted raw and blanched vegetables, such as bell peppers, broccoli, carrots, cauliflower, cherry tomatoes, cucumbers, and scallions

Heat oven to 350°F. Place pita wedges on a baking sheet and bake until crisp, 10 to 12 minutes.

Purée chickpeas, cannellini beans, tomatoes plus 1 tablespoon of their oil, and garlic in a food processor. Add yogurt, lemon juice, sesame oil, cumin, and salt; process until smooth. Serve at room temperature with pita triangles and vegetables for dipping.

Makes 2 cups and 32 pita chips

NUTRITION AT A GLANCE

Per tablespoon dip: 25 calories, 0.5 g fat, 0 g saturated fat, 1 g protein, 4 g carbohydrate, 0 g fiber, 65 mg sodium

Per 4 pita triangles: 170 calories, 1.5 g fat, 0 g saturated fat, 6 g protein, 35 g carbohydrate, 5 g fiber, 340 mg sodium

MAKE-AHEAD: The flavors of hummus improve when it's made up to 3 days in advance; refrigerate in a covered container until ready to use. Bring to room temperature before serving. Pita chips can be toasted up to a day ahead.

Garlicky Eggplant Dip

PREP TIME: 10 minutes   **COOK TIME:** 1 hour

The soft, creamy texture of cooked eggplant is perfect for blending into a dip. This one, flavored with onions, garlic, and lemon juice, will have your guests cheering for you.

- ¼ cup extra-virgin olive oil
- 1 large onion, coarsely chopped
- 4 garlic cloves, lightly smashed and peeled
- ¼ teaspoon crushed red pepper flakes, or more to taste
- 1 (2-pound) eggplant, coarsely chopped
- ¼ teaspoon salt
- Freshly ground black pepper
- ¼ cup fresh lemon juice
- Assorted raw and blanched vegetables, such as bell peppers, broccoli, cauliflower, cherry tomatoes, cucumbers, and scallions

Heat oil in a large saucepan over medium heat. Add onion, garlic, and pepper flakes; reduce heat to medium-low and cook until vegetables are softened, 5 to 7 minutes. Stir in eggplant, salt, and a pinch of black pepper. Cover and cook, stirring occasionally, until eggplant is very soft, 25 to 30 minutes. Transfer eggplant mixture to a large bowl and allow to cool for 15 minutes.

When cooled, process eggplant in a food processor or in batches in a blender until smooth, 1 to 2 minutes, adding lemon juice during the final 30 seconds of processing. Serve at room temperature with assorted vegetables for dipping.

Makes 2 cups

NUTRITION AT A GLANCE
Per tablespoon: 25 calories, 2 g fat, 0 g saturated fat, 0 g protein, 2 g carbohydrate, 1 g fiber, 20 mg sodium

MAKE-AHEAD: Dip can be made up to 8 hours ahead; refrigerate in a covered container and bring to room temperature before serving.

Buffalo Chicken Bites

PREP TIME: 15 minutes   **COOK TIME:** 10 minutes

What would a good football game be without the familiar taste of the devilishly spicy chicken that hails from upstate New York?

> 3   tablespoons trans-fat-free margarine
>
> 2   tablespoons hot pepper sauce, or more to taste
>
> 1   teaspoon canola oil
>
> 3   (6-ounce) boneless, skinless chicken breasts, cut into 24 (1-inch) cubes
>
> ¼   teaspoon salt
>
> ⅛   teaspoon freshly ground black pepper
>
> 3   celery stalks, cut into 24 (1-inch) pieces
>
>   Blue Cheese Dipping Sauce (opposite page)

Melt margarine in a medium nonstick saucepan. Whisk in pepper sauce and cook for 1 to 2 minutes, or until slightly thickened; set aside.

Heat oil in a large nonstick skillet over medium-high heat. Season chicken with salt and pepper, add to pan, and cook, turning occasionally, until browned on all sides, about 6 minutes. Add margarine mixture to pan and gently toss chicken until well coated, 1 to 2 minutes.

Remove chicken from pan and skewer each cube with a toothpick. Skewer 1 piece of celery at the base of each. Arrange on a platter and serve with dip.

Makes 8 (3-skewer) servings

NUTRITION AT A GLANCE

Per serving with 1 tablespoon dip: 150 calories, 9 g fat, 2.5 g saturated fat, 16 g protein, 1 g carbohydrate, 0 g fiber, 250 mg sodium

Blue Cheese Dipping Sauce

PREP TIME: 5 minutes

Buffalo chicken is especially delicious with a healthy blue cheese dip to help cool things off.

2 tablespoons crumbled blue cheese

¼ cup reduced-fat sour cream

2 tablespoons mayonnaise

1 teaspoon fresh lemon juice

1 teaspoon red wine vinegar

Hot pepper sauce

Mash blue cheese in a medium bowl, leaving some small lumps. Whisk in the sour cream, mayonnaise, lemon juice, vinegar, and pepper sauce to taste. Transfer to a small bowl and serve with the chicken.

Makes ½ cup

NUTRITION AT A GLANCE

Per tablespoon: 45 calories, 4.5 g fat, 1.5 g saturated fat, 1 g protein, 0 g carbohydrate, 0 g fiber, 55 mg sodium

MAKE-AHEAD: Dip can be made up to 1 day ahead; refrigerate in a covered container and serve chilled or at room temperature.

TIP **More uses for Blue Cheese Dipping Sauce:** This tasty sauce is wonderfully versatile. Try it as a dip for crudités; thin it out with a touch of fat-free milk for a salad dressing to use atop Romaine or arugula; or enjoy it as a sauce for sliced grilled steak.

Pork and Poblano Chili

PREP TIME: 20 minutes   **COOK TIME:** 2 hours 40 minutes

This "verde" or green-style chili gets full-bodied flavor and a nice hit of heat from a mixture of peppers. (You can substitute Anaheim or bell peppers for the poblanos.) Low-fat, high-flavor boneless pork loin roast is your best bet for good value; pork round cutlet and loin chops are also good. Many butchers will cut the pork for you.

1½ pounds poblano peppers (8 to 10 peppers), seeded and roughly chopped	4 pounds lean pork, cut into ¾-inch pieces
1 large onion, coarsely chopped	2 cups lower-sodium chicken broth
1 large green bell pepper, roughly chopped	1 (28-ounce) can unsalted diced tomatoes, with liquid
1 jalapeño, seeded and chopped	2 teaspoons ground cumin
6 garlic cloves, peeled	2 (15-ounce) cans cannellini beans, rinsed and drained
1 tablespoon extra-virgin olive oil	

Pulse poblano peppers in a food processor until finely chopped but not puréed; transfer to a large bowl. Pulse onion, bell pepper, jalapeño, and garlic in food processor until finely chopped but not puréed. Strain to remove any excess liquid and combine vegetables with poblano peppers.

Heat oil in a large, heavy-bottomed saucepan or Dutch oven over medium-high heat. Add pepper mixture, reduce heat to medium, and cook, stirring occasionally, until vegetables are well softened, 10 to 12 minutes. Stir in pork, broth, tomatoes and their liquid, and cumin. Bring to a simmer, partially cover, reduce heat to low, and simmer gently, stirring occasionally, until pork is very tender, about 2 hours. Add beans and cook until heated through, about 10 minutes more. Serve hot or warm.

Makes 16 (1-cup) servings

NUTRITION AT A GLANCE

Per serving: 220 calories, 6 g fat, 1.5 g saturated fat, 27 g protein, 14 g carbohydrate, 5 g fiber, 230 mg sodium

MAKE-AHEAD: Chili is best made 1 to 3 days before serving, since the flavor builds as it sits. Refrigerate in a covered container and gently reheat when ready to serve.

Eggless Tex-Mex Caesar Salad

PREP TIME: 15 minutes

Avocado, cilantro, and a dash of chili powder take a normal Caesar salad to new heights. Dress this salad in two or three batches if you don't have an extra-large salad bowl. Remember that anchovies are preserved in salt, so go light with extra seasoning.

1	plum tomato
3	anchovy fillets
2	garlic cloves, peeled
2	tablespoons fresh lemon juice
1	teaspoon Dijon mustard
¾	teaspoon chili powder
¼	cup extra-virgin olive oil
2	(½-pound) heads romaine lettuce, chopped (16 cups)
	Salt and freshly ground black pepper
2	avocados, pitted and cut into ¼-inch cubes
1	cup fresh cilantro leaves

Core tomato and make an X in the skin on the opposite end. Bring a small saucepan of water to a boil. Place tomato in boiling water and cook just until skin starts to pull away from flesh, about 30 seconds. Remove from water and drain. When tomato is cool enough to handle, peel off and discard skin.

Purée tomato, anchovy fillets, garlic, lemon juice, mustard, and chili powder in a food processor or blender. With machine running, add oil in a slow and steady stream; blend until incorporated.

Place lettuce in a large bowl; season lightly with salt and pepper. Add dressing and toss. Top with avocado, sprinkle with cilantro leaves, and serve.

Makes 10 (2-cup) servings

NUTRITION AT A GLANCE

Per serving: 120 calories, 11 g fat, 1.5 g saturated fat, 2 g protein, 6 g carbohydrate, 4 g fiber, 65 mg sodium

MAKE-AHEAD: Dressing can be made up to 1 day ahead. Refrigerate in a covered container and bring to room temperature before using.

Ranger Cookies

PREP TIME: 15 minutes   **COOK TIME:** 20 minutes

The true origin of this multiflavored cookie is unknown, but it is said that it's named for park and forest rangers who appreciated its energy-boosting ingredients.

¼ cup pecan pieces

¼ cup 100% bran cereal

¼ cup old-fashioned rolled oats

¼ cup bittersweet chocolate chips

¼ cup unsweetened coconut flakes

½ cup whole-grain pastry flour

¼ teaspoon baking powder

¼ teaspoon salt

½ cup trans-fat-free margarine

¼ cup granular sugar substitute

1 large egg

1 tablespoon vanilla extract

Heat oven to 375°F. Lightly coat a baking sheet with cooking spray or line with parchment.

Place pecans on another baking sheet and bake until fragrant and lightly toasted, 6 to 8 minutes. Remove from oven and set aside to cool briefly. Pulse cooled pecans, bran cereal, oats, chocolate chips, and coconut in a blender or food processor until coarsely ground.

Sift together flour, baking powder, and salt in a medium bowl. In a large bowl, with an electric mixer at high speed, beat margarine, sugar substitute, egg, and vanilla until creamy. With mixer on low, slowly add flour mixture to sugar mixture and beat until incorporated. Stir in pecan mixture.

Drop well-rounded tablespoons of batter 2 inches apart onto prepared baking sheet. Bake until tops of cookies appear dry and bottoms are golden, about 10 minutes. Transfer cookies to a wire rack to cool.

Makes 16 cookies

NUTRITION AT A GLANCE
Per cookie: 110 calories, 8 g fat, 2.5 g saturated fat, 1 g protein, 7 g carbohydrate, 1 g fiber, 95 mg sodium

MAKE-AHEAD: Cookies can be made 1 day ahead and stored in an airtight container at room temperature.

TUSCAN FEAST

FOR 6 GUESTS

In true Tuscan form, this easygoing menu is filled with lovely rustic fare. Italian seasonings, such as rosemary, garlic, and fennel, enhance scrumptious warm olives and a gorgeous rolled pork roast. There's also a classic bread salad updated South Beach Diet–style with the addition of whole-grain bread cubes and plenty of vegetables. And for dessert, feather-light lemony cheesecake.

Just as nice served indoors as it would be al fresco, this meal is especially tasty in the summer and early fall, when eggplant and peppers are at the height of their season. To keep the tone of the party relaxed and intimate, use colored glassware, informal ceramic dishes, and cloth napkins. Votive candles and bright, bold cut flowers can be placed throughout the house to add to the mood. You can serve the meal family-style, if you prefer: Passing big plates and bowls piled high with good food from guest to guest expresses the warmth and conviviality of the Italian way of life.

◀ *Serve this Tuscan feast in early to midafternoon (as the Italians do) and encourage guests to linger at the table as long as they like.*

MENU

Roasted Eggplant and Peppers

Marinated Olives

Panzanella Salad

Herb-Roasted Pork Loin

Warm White Beans with Rosemary

Ricotta Cheesecake with Lemon Drizzle and Pine Nuts

Party Game Plan

Up to 3 days before: Toast bread cubes for salad.

Up to 1 day before: Marinate olives; rub and tie pork; prepare beans; make cake.

Day of: Roast pork; assemble salad; roast vegetables; heat beans.

Roasted Eggplant and Peppers

PREP TIME: 10 minutes   **COOK TIME: 40 minutes**

Most of the time required to prepare this delicious dish is when the vegetables are roasting, which frees you up to set the table and complete last-minute preparations.

1 pound eggplant	1 tablespoon plus 1 teaspoon extra-virgin olive oil
2 large red bell peppers, cut into 1½-inch-wide strips	Salt and freshly ground black pepper
1 medium onion, cut into wedges	

Heat oven to 450°F. Line 2 baking sheets with parchment or foil.

Cut eggplant in half crosswise, then cut each half into 8 to 10 wedges, ¾-inch thick at the widest spot. Combine eggplant, peppers, and onion in a large bowl. Add oil and toss to coat. Season lightly with salt and pepper.

Spread vegetables on baking sheets. Using a spatula, scrape any remaining oil and seasonings from the bowl over the vegetables.

Roast vegetables, turning once, until softened and blistered on edges and bottoms, 35 to 40 minutes. Remove from oven and serve hot or warm.

Makes 6 servings

NUTRITION AT A GLANCE
Per serving: 70 calories, 3.5 g fat, 0.5 g saturated fat, 1 g protein, 9 g carbohydrate, 4 g fiber, 0 mg sodium

MAKE-AHEAD: Vegetables can be made up to 8 hours in advance. Cover with plastic wrap and leave at room temperature (do not refrigerate). Gently warm in oven before serving.

Marinated Olives

PREP TIME: 15 minutes   **COOK TIME: 5 minutes**

For a nice presentation, choose a mix of olives for this recipe. Some of our favorites are Cerignola, niçoise, kalamata, Moroccan oil-cured, and Sicilian green.

½ pound mixed olives	1 teaspoon dried basil
2 tablespoons extra-virgin olive oil	½ teaspoon grated orange zest
1 bay leaf	¼ teaspoon red pepper flakes

Combine olives, oil, bay leaf, basil, zest, and pepper flakes in a small saucepan. Cook over low heat, stirring occasionally, for 5 minutes. Remove from heat and let sit for at least 10 minutes before serving.

Makes 6 servings

Per serving: 90 calories, 10 g fat, 1 g saturated fat, 0 g protein, 3 g carbohydrate, 0 g fiber, 480 mg sodium

MAKE-AHEAD: Olives can be marinated up to 1 day ahead.

Panzanella Salad

PREP TIME: 15 minutes   COOK TIME: 15 minutes

A bountiful, rustic Italian bread salad, panzanella is as gorgeous to behold as it is tasty to eat. Be sure to use ripe, juicy tomatoes and all their juices.

3 thin slices whole-grain bread, cut into ¾-inch cubes	¾ pound hearts of romaine lettuce, chopped (8 cups)
1 small garlic clove, minced	2 large tomatoes, cut into chunks
⅛ teaspoon salt	1 small red onion, thinly sliced
3 tablespoons extra-virgin olive oil	½ cup packed fresh basil leaves
3 tablespoons red wine vinegar	Freshly ground black pepper

Heat oven to 350°F. Place bread cubes on a baking sheet; bake until golden and lightly toasted, about 12 minutes. Cool completely.

Meanwhile, mash garlic and salt together in a small bowl. Add oil and vinegar, and whisk to combine.

Combine lettuce, tomatoes, onion, basil, and toasted bread cubes in a large bowl. Toss with dressing. Season to taste, and serve.

Makes 6 (1½-cup) servings

Per serving: 120 calories, 8 g fat, 1 g saturated fat, 3 g protein, 13 g carbohydrate, 3 g fiber, 125 mg sodium

MAKE-AHEAD: Bread cubes can be toasted up to 3 days in advance; store at room temperature or refrigerate in an airtight container.

Herb-Roasted Pork Loin

PREP TIME: 20 minutes   **COOK TIME:** 1½ hours

This aromatic roast fills the kitchen with the scent of herbs, fennel, and garlic—a classic Tuscan combination. You can ask your butcher to double butterfly the loin for you, but it is also easy to do it at home, as we explain below.

6 garlic cloves, minced

2 teaspoons dried oregano

2 teaspoons fennel seeds

2 teaspoons finely grated lemon zest

1 teaspoon extra-virgin olive oil

¼ teaspoon salt

1 (3-pound) boneless center-cut pork loin roast

Position rack in middle of oven and heat oven to 350°F.

Combine garlic, oregano, fennel seeds, zest, oil, and salt in a small bowl. Mash until mixture forms a thick paste.

Place pork on a cutting board so it lies perpendicular to you. Using a sharp knife and beginning at the top of the loin, make an incision down the center, about three-quarters of the way into the meat. Gently spread the loin open and repeat the incision in the center of each half of the loin, so the loin is opened, like a book.

Rub three-fourths of the garlic mixture inside the loin, then close up the loin by folding in half and then in half again. Use twine to tie loin closed. Rub the remaining garlic mixture over the outside of the loin.

Roast pork until internal temperature reads 150°F, 1 to 1½ hours. Remove from oven and let rest 20 minutes before slicing; serve warm.

Makes 8 (6-ounce) servings

NUTRITION AT A GLANCE

Per serving: 230 calories, 8 g fat, 2.5 g saturated fat, 36 g protein, 1 g carbohydrate, 0 g fiber, 160 mg sodium

MAKE-AHEAD: Pork can be rubbed, tied, and refrigerated up to 1 day ahead.

Warm White Beans with Rosemary

PREP TIME: 5 minutes   **COOK TIME:** 10 minutes

When these fantastic beans arrive at the table, your guests will never guess that they took mere minutes to prepare. A few pantry ingredients and—presto!—a perfect side dish appears.

3 tablespoons extra-virgin olive oil	2 (15-ounce) cans cannellini beans, rinsed and drained
1 bay leaf	Freshly ground black pepper
1½ teaspoons dried rosemary, crushed	

Heat oil, bay leaf, and rosemary in a medium saucepan over medium heat until oil begins to bubble, 1 to 2 minutes. Reduce heat to low and cook 2 minutes more. Add beans and season with pepper to taste. Cover and cook until beans are heated through, about 5 minutes more. Discard bay leaf. Serve warm.

Makes 6 (½-cup) servings

NUTRITION AT A GLANCE
Per serving: 150 calories, 7 g fat, 1 g saturated fat, 6 g protein, 15 g carbohydrate, 6 g fiber, 320 mg sodium

MAKE-AHEAD: Recipe can be made up to 1 day in advance and refrigerated in a covered container. Gently reheat on stove top or in a microwave. Add an extra drizzle of extra-virgin olive oil if beans appear dry.

Ricotta Cheesecake with Lemon Drizzle and Pine Nuts

PREP TIME: 10 minutes   **COOK TIME:** 1 hour 20 minutes   **CHILL TIME:** 4 hours or overnight

This traditional Italian dessert is refreshingly light and delicately citrusy. You'll find it's quite unlike our dense, creamy American cheesecake, but no less delicious.

3 tablespoons pine nuts

6 large eggs, separated

¾ teaspoon cream of tartar

⅓ cup plus 1 teaspoon granular sugar substitute

2 teaspoons vanilla extract

1 (32-ounce) container part-skim ricotta cheese

1 teaspoon finely grated lemon zest

2 tablespoons fresh lemon juice

Position rack in middle of oven and heat oven to 275°F. Lightly coat a 9-inch springform pan with cooking spray. Spread nuts on a baking sheet and toast until lightly golden, about 10 minutes. Cool. Increase oven to 325°F.

In a large metal bowl, with an electric mixer at high speed, beat egg whites until frothy, about 1 minute. Add cream of tartar and continue to beat until stiff peaks form, about 3 minutes more. Set aside.

In a separate large bowl, beat egg yolks, ⅓ cup of the sugar substitute, and vanilla for 1 minute. Add ricotta and zest, and beat on high until smooth.

Gently fold one-third of the whites into the yolk mixture, then add the rest of the whites and gently fold until well combined. Pour batter into pan, place pan on a baking sheet, and bake until cake is golden and mostly set, about 1 hour 10 minutes. Remove cake from oven and cool on a rack for 20 minutes.

Combine lemon juice and remaining 1 teaspoon sugar substitute in a saucepan; bring to a simmer over low heat. Remove from heat and gently brush the surface of the cooled cake with two-thirds of the warm lemon mixture; drizzle the remaining mixture into the cracks. Sprinkle the top with pine nuts.

Cool cake completely, then run a knife around the edge before releasing from pan. Chill, loosely covered, for 4 hours or overnight. Serve chilled.

Makes 12 servings

NUTRITION AT A GLANCE
Per serving: 140 calories, 9 g fat, 4.5 g saturated fat, 11 g protein, 5 g carbohydrate, 0 g fiber, 140 mg sodium

MAKE-AHEAD: Cheesecake is best made 1 day ahead and refrigerated.

FRENCH BISTRO PARTY

FOR 6 GUESTS

Give your guests a taste of France with this charming meal. Although the dishes may sound fancy, they're surprisingly easy to make. Fresh mussels, prepared with herbs and white wine, require just five ingredients and only minutes to steam. If you've never made a cassoulet, there's nothing to fear, since this simple peasant fare is cooked just like a casserole. And tender Brussels sprouts, bathed in heart-healthy olive oil and roasted with garlic, will turn even the most persnickety eater into a fan.

To set the mood, play some classic French music by such singers as Serge Gainsbourg, Charles Aznavour, and Edith Piaf; they're great fun to listen to and their performances often show up together on compilation CDs. But most important, keep the party unfussy and comfortable. The critical factors in presenting a good French bistro meal are quality, healthful ingredients, and loving preparation. Focus on these and you'll get more than your fair share of "ooh la la!"

◄ *Mussels steamed with white wine and presented with frisée salad will quickly remind guests of France. A starfish on each napkin says South Beach.*

MENU

*Endive Spears with
Walnut Goat Cheese*

Steamed Mussels with White Wine

Chicken Cassoulet

Brussels Sprouts with Garlic

Frisée Salad with Toasted Almonds

*Warm Buckwheat Crêpes with
Mixed Berries*

Party Game Plan

Up to 3 days before: Toast walnuts for endive and almonds for salad; make crêpes.

Up to 2 days before: Make cassoulet.

Day of: Make goat cheese mixture for endive and sauce for crêpes; assemble endive spears and salad; steam mussels; roast Brussels sprouts; heat cassoulet; assemble crêpes.

Endive Spears with Walnut Goat Cheese

PREP TIME: 10 minutes   **COOK TIME:** 10 minutes

Toasting the walnuts gives deep flavor to this wonderful cheese spread, made a touch sweet with the addition of minced shallot. Spooned onto a crisp spear of endive, it's a gracious and sophisticated way to begin the party.

¼ cup walnut pieces

2 small heads Belgian endive

1 (3.5-ounce) package goat cheese, softened at room temperature

1 tablespoon minced shallot

⅛ teaspoon salt

   Freshly ground black pepper

Heat oven to 275°F. Place walnuts on a baking sheet and bake until fragrant and lightly toasted, about 10 minutes. Remove from oven; cool and finely chop.

Trim the base of endive heads and separate into leaves. Set aside the 18 largest leaves; save the remainder for another use.

Stir together walnuts, goat cheese, shallot, salt, and a pinch of pepper in a small bowl. Spoon rounded teaspoons of goat cheese mixture onto the wide ends of the endive leaves. Transfer to a platter and serve.

Makes 6 (3-piece) servings

NUTRITION AT A GLANCE
Per serving: 80 calories, 7 g fat, 2.5 g saturated fat, 4 g protein, 2 g carbohydrate, 0 g fiber, 110 mg sodium

MAKE-AHEAD: Walnuts can be toasted up to 3 days ahead and stored in an airtight container at room temperature or in the refrigerator. Goat cheese mixture can be made up to 8 hours ahead and stored in a covered container in the refrigerator; bring to room temperature before using. Endive spears can be assembled up to 2 hours before guests arrive; cover with plastic wrap, return to the refrigerator, and remove 15 minutes before the party begins.

Steamed Mussels with White Wine

PREP TIME: 15 minutes   **COOK TIME:** 15 minutes

Mussels are one of the simplest shellfish to cook and, visually, one of the most impressive. Low in calories, they're packed with protein and a host of vitamins and minerals, making them a healthy alternative to meat. Bringing this dish to the table, steaming right from the stove, creates dramatic effect. Place two or three empty bowls on the table for discarded shells. Since most of the wine evaporates during cooking, this is a fine Phase 1 dish.

- 2 tablespoons extra-virgin olive oil
- 2 garlic cloves, thinly sliced
- 3 pounds mussels, cleaned
- ⅓ cup white wine
- 2 tablespoons fresh thyme leaves or 2 teaspoons dried thyme

Heat oil in a large nonstick saucepan over medium heat. Add garlic and cook, stirring occasionally, until translucent, about 3 minutes. Add mussels, wine, and thyme; stir and cover. Steam mussels until they open, about 8 minutes, stirring halfway through cooking.

Remove mussels from the pot, discarding any that haven't opened, and transfer to a large serving bowl. Pour cooking liquid over mussels. Serve hot with a few tablespoons of broth for each serving.

Makes 6 servings

NUTRITION AT A GLANCE
Per serving: 180 calories, 8 g fat, 1.5 g saturated fat, 18 g protein, 6 g carbohydrate, 0 g fiber, 430 mg sodium

Chicken Cassoulet

PREP TIME: 20 minutes   **COOK TIME: 1 hour 10 minutes**

Fragrant and bubbling, our version of this rustic French country dish uses chicken breast, which provides great flavor without the added fat of the traditional duck or goose.

6 (6-ounce) boneless, skinless chicken breasts, cut in half	1½ teaspoons dried thyme
Salt and black pepper	2 tablespoons unsalted tomato paste
2 tablespoons extra-virgin olive oil	½ cup white wine
1 medium onion, chopped	1 (15.5-ounce) can cannellini beans, rinsed and drained
3 garlic cloves, minced	1 (14.5-ounce) can unsalted diced tomatoes
3 small rutabagas or turnips, peeled and diced (1¼ pounds)	1 cup lower-sodium chicken broth
3 medium carrots, thinly sliced	¼ cup chopped fresh parsley
3 celery stalks, chopped	

Heat oven to 425°F.

Season chicken with salt and pepper. Heat 1 tablespoon of the oil in a large nonstick skillet over medium-high heat. Add chicken and cook until lightly browned, about 5 minutes per side. Transfer chicken to a plate and set aside.

Reduce heat to medium and add remaining 1 tablespoon oil to the skillet. Add onion and garlic, and cook, stirring occasionally, until softened and lightly browned, about 6 minutes. Add rutabagas, carrots, celery, and thyme, and cook, stirring occasionally, until vegetables are lightly browned, about 10 minutes. Stir in tomato paste and cook for 3 minutes, stirring frequently.

Increase heat to medium-high and add wine. Simmer until most of the liquid has evaporated, about 2 minutes. Add beans and tomatoes; cook until bubbling, about 2 minutes. Add broth and bring to a simmer.

Transfer cassoulet to a large casserole dish and bake until browned and bubbling, 30 to 35 minutes. Sprinkle with parsley.

Makes 6 servings

NUTRITION AT A GLANCE
Per serving: 330 calories, 7 g fat, 1 g saturated fat, 44 g protein, 19 g carbohydrate, 5 g fiber, 400 mg sodium

MAKE-AHEAD: The entire recipe can be made up to 2 days ahead; refrigerate, covered, in the casserole dish until ready to use. Reheat, covered, in a warm oven.

Brussels Sprouts with Garlic

PREP TIME: 10 minutes   **COOK TIME:** 25 minutes

Even the most skeptical guest will fall for these delectable Brussels sprouts, made extremely moist and tender with the addition of water during roasting. Use good-quality olive oil and fresh garlic.

- 1 pound Brussels sprouts, halved
- 3 garlic cloves, thinly sliced
- 1 tablespoon plus 1 teaspoon extra-virgin olive oil
- ¼ teaspoon salt
  Freshly ground black pepper
- ½ cup water

Heat oven to 425°F.

Place Brussels sprouts, garlic, oil, salt, and a pinch of pepper in a 9- by 13-inch baking dish; toss to coat. Spread out in a single layer. Pour the water into the dish and roast until Brussels sprouts are lightly browned and pierced easily with a paring knife, about 25 minutes. Serve warm.

Makes 6 servings

NUTRITION AT A GLANCE

Per serving: 60 calories, 3.5 g fat, 0 g saturated fat, 3 g protein, 7 g carbohydrate, 3 g fiber, 115 mg sodium

MAKE-AHEAD: You can combine all the elements of this dish, except the water, up to 8 hours before roasting. Cover and leave at room temperature. Remember to uncover and add the water before placing in the oven.

TIP **Buying and storing Brussels sprouts:** Fresh Brussels sprouts are widely available from late August through March. Look for bright green leaves and firm heads. Store Brussels sprouts unwashed in an airtight plastic bag for up to 3 days.

Frisée Salad with Toasted Almonds

PREP TIME: 15 minutes   **BAKE TIME:** 10 minutes

Delicate and frilly, frisée is a classic French green that offers a surprising array of nutritional benefits. Rich in beta-carotene, vitamin C, and potassium, the tender lettuce also provides calcium, iron, and magnesium. If you can't find frisée, make this salad with a mix of torn dark green leaf lettuce and radicchio.

3 tablespoons slivered almonds	1 tablespoon red wine vinegar
1 large cucumber, peeled	1 teaspoon Dijon mustard
1 (10-ounce) head frisée, torn into bite-size pieces (about 7 cups)	2 tablespoons extra-virgin olive oil
Salt and freshly ground black pepper	

Heat oven to 275°F. Spread almonds on a baking sheet and bake until fragrant and lightly toasted, 8 to 10 minutes. Remove from oven and cool.

Cut cucumber in half lengthwise, seed, and slice into half-moons. Combine cucumber, frisée, almonds, and salt and pepper to taste in a large serving bowl.

Whisk together vinegar and mustard in a small bowl; slowly whisk in oil. Pour dressing over greens, toss to coat, and serve.

Makes 6 servings

NUTRITION AT A GLANCE
Per serving: 70 calories, 6 g fat, 1 g saturated fat, 1 g protein, 3 g carbohydrate, 2 g fiber, 20 mg sodium

MAKE-AHEAD: Almonds can be toasted up to 3 days ahead and stored in a covered container in the refrigerator.

Warm Buckwheat Crêpes with Mixed Berries

PREP TIME: 20 minutes   **COOK TIME:** 30 minutes

Buckwheat flour has a nutty taste that adds flavorful depth to these beautiful crêpes. Use an 8-inch skillet when making this dish.

3 tablespoons buckwheat flour	½ teaspoon granular sugar substitute
2 tablespoons unbleached all-purpose flour	⅛ teaspoon ground cinnamon
¼ cup fat-free milk	⅛ teaspoon grated lemon zest
1 large egg	Salt
2 teaspoons canola oil	1½ cups mixed frozen berries, thawed
1 tablespoon plus 1½ teaspoons warm water	

Purée buckwheat and all-purpose flours, milk, egg, oil, water, sugar substitute, cinnamon, zest, and a pinch of salt in a blender until smooth, about 1 minute. Set aside to rest for 15 minutes. Meanwhile, place berries in a small saucepan and cook over medium-low heat until gently bubbling and warmed through. Remove from heat and cover pan to keep warm.

Lightly coat the skillet with cooking spray and heat over medium heat. Add 2 tablespoons of the batter, tilting the pan so that batter forms an even, thin layer. Cook until bubbles form and edges begin to brown, about 1 minute. Using a spatula, carefully flip the crêpe over and cook until golden on the bottom, about 1 minute. Transfer crêpe, golden side down, to a plate. Repeat with remaining batter, coating the pan with cooking spray after each crêpe. Stack crêpes as you go.

To serve, place 1 crêpe, golden side down, on a plate. Place 2 tablespoons berries in the center and roll up crêpe around berries. Spoon 2 more tablespoons berries and some juices over the top. Repeat with remaining crêpes. Serve warm or at room temperature.

Makes 6 crêpes

NUTRITION AT A GLANCE
Per crêpe: 70 calories, 2.5 g fat, 0 g saturated fat, 2 g protein, 9 g carbohydrate, 2 g fiber, 15 mg sodium

MAKE-AHEAD: Crêpes can be made up to 3 days ahead and stored, tightly wrapped in one pile, in the refrigerator. Gently reheat in a microwave on low for 15 seconds or in a warm oven.

BACKYARD GRILL FEST

FOR 10 GUESTS

Friends and family of all ages are sure to enjoy this festive outdoor meal on a hot summer day. A refreshing chilled gazpacho is enhanced with the bold flavors of sweet roasted red peppers. Salmon is gussied up with a ginger marinade. And grilled chicken (a second main course option) gets a lift from a tasty blend of Indian spices. We've also included a seasonal bounty of vitamin-rich veggies, in every color imaginable, including juicy tomatoes, crunchy radishes, and crisp cucumbers. And for dessert, there's an old-fashioned cobbler made with blueberries, one of our favorite healthy fruits.

Simple tableware is best when it comes to dining outside. Keep it casual with colorful plastic or melamine plates and cups. You can roll up the silverware in oversized napkins and tie them with different-colored ribbons, then place the bundles in a pretty basket on your buffet, if you'd like.

◂*A buffet is just right for the casual nature of a backyard party. You can grill the salmon, chicken, and vegetables indoors if the weather suddenly shifts.*

MENU

Roasted Pepper Gazpacho

Grilled Ginger Salmon

Radish and Jícama Salad

Grilled Vegetable Skewers

Indian-Spiced Grilled Chicken

Three-Grain Tabouli

Blueberry Cobbler

Party Game Plan

Up to 2 days before: Prepare grains for tabouli.

Up to 1 day before: Make gazpacho; marinate salmon, chicken, and vegetables.

Day of: Prepare and bake cobbler; assemble tabouli; make salad; grill salmon, chicken, and vegetables.

Roasted Pepper Gazpacho

PREP TIME: 20 minutes   **CHILL TIME: 2 hours**

Roasted peppers bring a sweet earthy flavor to gazpacho that's at once unexpected and remarkably flavorful. If you can't find the yellow peppers, simply use all red.

1 (12-ounce) jar roasted red peppers, drained and roughly chopped

1 (12-ounce) jar roasted yellow peppers, drained and roughly chopped

1 (14.5-ounce) can diced tomatoes

2 cucumbers, peeled, seeded, and roughly chopped

1 small red onion, roughly chopped

1 small jalapeño, seeded and roughly chopped

3 garlic cloves, roughly chopped

2 cups low-sodium tomato juice

2 tablespoons extra-virgin olive oil

2 tablespoons red wine vinegar

¼ teaspoon salt

⅛ teaspoon freshly ground black pepper

Pulse red and yellow peppers, tomatoes, cucumbers, onion, jalapeño, and garlic in a food processor until mixture is still slightly chunky. Add tomato juice, oil, vinegar, salt, and pepper; pulse until just combined.

Transfer gazpacho to a large bowl, cover, and refrigerate for at least 2 hours or overnight. Serve chilled.

Makes 10 (¾-cup) servings

NUTRITION AT A GLANCE
Per serving: 80 calories, 3 g fat, 0 g saturated fat, 1 g protein, 13 g carbohydrate, 1 g fiber, 270 mg sodium

MAKE-AHEAD: Gazpacho can be made up to 1 day in advance; refrigerate, covered, until ready to serve.

Grilled Ginger Salmon

PREP TIME: 10 minutes   **MARINATING TIME:** 2 hours or overnight   **COOK TIME:** 10 minutes

You don't have to marinate this pleasantly peppery, Asian-style salmon for more than an hour, but the more time you can give it, the more flavorful it will be. Marinate overnight, if you can.

⅓ cup canola oil

3 tablespoons minced fresh ginger

1 tablespoon light soy sauce

2 garlic cloves, minced

10 (6-ounce) salmon fillets, about 1 inch thick

Whisk together oil, ginger, soy sauce, and garlic in a small bowl; divide marinade between 2 large resealable plastic bags. Place 5 fillets in each bag, seal bags, and turn to coat salmon with marinade. Lay bags flat in the refrigerator. Refrigerate at least 2 hours or overnight, turning once.

Heat a grill or grill pan to medium-high. Remove salmon from bags and grill until medium-rare, about 5 minutes per side. Serve warm.

Makes 10 (6-ounce) servings

NUTRITION AT A GLANCE

Per serving: 380 calories, 26 g fat, 4 g saturated fat, 34 g protein, 1 g carbohydrate, 0 g fiber, 160 mg sodium

MAKE-AHEAD: Salmon can be marinated in resealable plastic bags in the refrigerator up to 1 day in advance.

TIP **Peeling ginger:** Use the edge of a teaspoon to scrape the peel off the ginger; it's easier than using a conventional vegetable peeler.

Radish and Jícama Salad

PREP TIME: 20 minutes

Refreshing and crisp, this salad gets additional crunch from jícama and great flavor from the lime and lemon juices, scallions, and cilantro.

¾ pound radishes, thinly sliced (about 4 cups)

1 pound jícama, julienned (about 4 cups)

1 bunch scallions, thinly sliced

3 tablespoons extra-virgin olive oil

1 tablespoon fresh lime juice

2 teaspoons fresh lemon juice

¼ teaspoon salt

3 tablespoons chopped fresh cilantro

Combine radishes, jícama, and scallions in a large serving bowl.

Whisk oil, lime and lemon juices, and salt together in a small bowl. Pour dressing over vegetables and toss. Add cilantro and toss again. Serve at room temperature.

Makes 10 (¾-cup) servings

NUTRITION AT A GLANCE

Per serving: 60 calories, 4.5 g fat, 0.5 g saturated fat, 1 g protein, 6 g carbohydrate, 0 g fiber, 70 mg sodium

MAKE-AHEAD: Salad can be prepared (except for cilantro) up to 6 hours in advance; cover and refrigerate until ready to serve. Add cilantro just before serving.

Grilled Vegetable Skewers

PREP TIME: 20 minutes   **MARINATING TIME:** 30 minutes or overnight   **COOK TIME:** 10 minutes

Lemon, garlic, and olive oil add great flavor to these healthy skewers. If you use wooden skewers soak them for 10 minutes before using.

4 medium zucchini (about 2 pounds), cut into 40 (¾-inch) pieces

20 button mushrooms

2 medium yellow summer squash (about 1 pound), cut into 20 (¾-inch) pieces

½ cup extra-virgin olive oil

2 tablespoons fresh lemon juice

4 garlic cloves, minced

¼ teaspoon salt

¼ teaspoon freshly ground black pepper

Lemon wedges

Alternating the vegetables, thread 1 piece of zucchini, 1 mushroom, 1 piece of summer squash, and another piece of zucchini onto each of 20 (6-inch) skewers. Place skewers in a single layer in a baking dish.

Whisk together oil, lemon juice, garlic, salt, and pepper in a small bowl. Pour marinade over vegetable skewers. Marinate 30 minutes at room temperature or overnight, covered, in the refrigerator, turning several times.

Heat a grill or grill pan to medium-high. Grill vegetable skewers, turning several times, until vegetables are cooked and lightly charred, about 8 minutes. Serve warm or at room temperature with lemon wedges.

Makes 10 (2-skewer) servings

NUTRITION AT A GLANCE
Per serving: 80 calories, 6 g fat, 1 g saturated fat, 2 g protein, 6 g carbohydrate, 2 g fiber, 70 mg sodium

MAKE-AHEAD: Vegetables can be marinated on the skewers in a covered pan and refrigerated up to 1 day in advance.

Indian-Spiced Grilled Chicken

PREP TIME: 10 minutes   **MARINATING TIME:** 2 hours or overnight   **COOK TIME:** 15 minutes

Lightly smoky, spicy, and juicy, this scrumptious chicken is flavored with garam masala, a classic Indian spice mixture (garam means "warm" or "hot") that varies in makeup but often contains ground black pepper, cinnamon, cloves, coriander, cumin, cardamom, dried chilies, fennel, mace, and nutmeg. Look for it in the spice section of your supermarket or mix up your own combination using as many of the spices listed above as you'd like.

¾ cup plain nonfat or low-fat yogurt

2 tablespoons fresh lemon juice

4 teaspoons garam masala

2 teaspoons paprika

¼ teaspoon salt

⅛ teaspoon freshly ground black pepper

⅛ teaspoon cayenne pepper

10 (6-ounce) boneless, skinless chicken breasts

1 tablespoon vegetable oil

Whisk together yogurt, lemon juice, garam masala, paprika, salt, black pepper, and cayenne in a small bowl. Divide mixture between 2 large resealable plastic bags. Place 5 chicken breasts in each bag, seal bags, and turn to coat chicken with marinade. Lay bags flat in the refrigerator. Refrigerate at least 2 hours or overnight.

Heat a grill or grill pan to medium-high. Remove chicken from bags. Brush grill with oil and grill chicken until cooked through, about 7 minutes per side. Serve warm.

Makes 10 (6-ounce) servings

NUTRITION AT A GLANCE
Per serving: 210 calories, 3.5 g fat, 0.5 g saturated fat, 40 g protein, 2 g carbohydrate, 0 g fiber, 180 mg sodium

MAKE-AHEAD: Chicken can be marinated in resealable plastic bags in the refrigerator up to 1 day in advance.

Three-Grain Tabouli

PREP TIME: 1 hour   **COOK TIME:** 10 minutes

This terrific twist on traditional tabouli combines bulgur, quinoa, and couscous with crisp cucumber and celery, tangy lemon juice, and juicy tomato to make a wonderful salad that beautifully complements both the grilled chicken and salmon.

½ cup bulgur

½ cup quinoa

⅓ cup whole-wheat couscous

2 cups finely chopped fresh parsley

1 medium cucumber, seeded and diced

1 medium tomato, finely chopped

2 celery stalks, diced

¼ cup extra-virgin olive oil

3 tablespoons fresh lemon juice

½ teaspoon salt

Place bulgur in a medium bowl. Add 1 cup of boiling water and cover. Allow to sit at room temperature for 45 minutes.

Meanwhile, bring another 1 cup water to a boil in a small saucepan. Add quinoa and stir. Cover and simmer for 10 minutes, remove from heat, and transfer to a large serving bowl.

In another medium bowl, combine couscous and 1 cup boiling water. Cover and allow to sit for 5 minutes. Transfer to bowl with quinoa.

Combine bulgur with quinoa and couscous. Stir in parsley, cucumber, tomato, celery, oil, lemon juice, and salt. Serve at room temperature.

Makes 14 (½-cup) servings

NUTRITION AT A GLANCE
Per serving: 90 calories, 4.5 g fat, 0 g saturated fat, 2 g protein, 12 g carbohydrate, 2 g fiber, 90 mg sodium

MAKE-AHEAD: All three grains can be prepared up to 2 days in advance; cool completely before refrigerating together in a covered container until ready to use. Toss with vegetables and seasonings up to 6 hours before guests arrive, and bring to room temperature before serving.

Blueberry Cobbler

PREP TIME: 10 minutes   **COOK TIME:** 40 minutes

Everyone loves a fruit cobbler made with blueberries, especially at an outdoor party on a warm summer day. Low in calories, high in fiber, and wonderfully sweet, blueberries also contain more disease-fighting antioxidants than practically any other fruit or vegetable.

- 4 pints fresh blueberries or 4 (12-ounce) bags frozen blueberries (not thawed)
- ¼ cup plus 2 tablespoons granular sugar substitute
- 2 cups whole-grain pastry flour
- 1 tablespoon baking powder
- 1 teaspoon ground cinnamon
- ½ cup plus 2 tablespoons trans-fat-free margarine, chilled
- ¾ cup plus 2 tablespoons 1% milk

Heat oven to 375°F.

Toss blueberries with ¼ cup of the sugar substitute in a large bowl. Place mixture in a 9- by 13-inch baking dish.

Combine flour with remaining 2 tablespoons sugar substitute, baking powder, and cinnamon. Add margarine and, using a pastry blender or 2 knives, cut in until mixture resembles coarse meal. Stir in ¾ cup of the milk to make a slightly sticky, soft dough.

Drop the dough by large spoonfuls over the fruit, covering as much of the fruit as you can. Brush dough with remaining 2 tablespoons milk. Bake until topping is golden and berries are hot and bubbling, 35 to 40 minutes. Serve warm.

Makes 12 servings

NUTRITION AT A GLANCE
Per serving: 210 calories, 9 g fat, 2.5 g saturated fat, 3 g protein, 31 g carbohydrate, 5 g fiber, 210 mg sodium

MAKE-AHEAD: Cobbler can be made up to 8 hours ahead and reheated in a 325°F oven until heated through.

HORS D'OEUVRES FOR A CROWD

FOR 10 GUESTS

Nothing gets good conversation flowing like a casual affair filled with an array of fine finger foods. Here you'll find healthy choices that don't miss a beat when it comes to nutritious ingredients and innovative touches.

Deviled eggs and a delectably smooth salmon mousse taste just like the classics, yet they're lightened with low-fat yogurt and reduced-fat sour cream. Baked sweet potato rounds filled with feta cheese and delicious roasted zucchini sprinkled with Parmesan provide appealing vegetarian options. And mini cannoli tartlets made with whole-wheat phyllo (and bittersweet chocolate, of course) deliver a world of sweet satisfaction in just a few bites.

For ease, set out the chilled foods buffet-style prior to party time, then bring out warm items as soon as guests arrive. You can also ask a friend to help out in the kitchen before or during the party and even pass certain items as well.

◀ *Throwing a party with so many menu options takes some advance planning, but most of the dishes can be made ahead.*

MENU

Smoked Trout Salad in Cherry Tomato Cups

Spicy Citrus Shrimp

Deviled Eggs

Salmon Mousse

Parmesan Zucchini Sticks

Sweet Potato–Feta Rounds

Chocolate-Dipped Strawberries

Cannoli Tartlets

Raspberry-Ginger Fizzes

Party Game Plan

Up to 3 days before: Toast walnuts and sesame seeds for strawberries.

Up to 2 days before: Hard-boil eggs.

Up to 1 day before: Make trout salad; marinate shrimp; make salmon mousse; cut up zucchini sticks; prepare cheese mixture for sweet potatoes; make cannoli filling; make raspberry-ginger fizz base.

Day of: Dip strawberries; grill shrimp; assemble deviled eggs; fill tomato cups and cannoli tartlets; bake sweet potato rounds and zucchini sticks; make fizzes.

Smoked Trout Salad in Cherry Tomato Cups

PREP TIME: 20 minutes

Rich, smoky trout in little tomato "cups" makes a festive, easy-to-eat combination. You can use both red and yellow cherry tomatoes, if desired.

¼ pound smoked trout (remove skin if necessary)

2 tablespoons reduced-fat sour cream

1 tablespoon fresh lemon juice

1 tablespoon chopped fresh chives

Freshly ground black pepper

30 large cherry tomatoes (1 pint)

Chopped fresh chives for garnish (optional)

Place trout in a medium bowl and break up into small pieces with a fork. Add sour cream, lemon juice, and chives; stir to combine. Season generously with pepper.

Using a serrated knife, cut ⅛ inch off the stem end of each tomato and a tiny bit off the bottom so the tomatoes will stand. Remove the seeds using a small melon baller. Fill each hollow tomato with a generous ½ teaspoon of the trout salad. Sprinkle each with a few chives, if using, and serve.

Makes 10 (3-piece) servings

NUTRITION AT A GLANCE
Per serving: 40 calories, 2 g fat, 0.5 g saturated fat, 3 g protein, 3 g carbohydrate, 0 g fiber, 75 mg sodium

MAKE-AHEAD: Trout salad can be made up to 1 day in advance; refrigerate in a covered container and bring to room temperature before using. Tomatoes can be hollowed out up to 1 hour before the party; cover with plastic wrap but do not refrigerate. Fill shortly before serving.

Spicy Citrus Shrimp

PREP TIME: 15 minutes   **MARINATING TIME:** 30 minutes or overnight   **COOK TIME:** 10 minutes

Lemon and orange liven up these garlicky shrimp, made spicy with a bit of red pepper flakes. Add more pepper flakes to your liking or sprinkle the marinade mixture with a few drops of hot sauce or pepper oil, if you dare! This recipe becomes Phase 1 if you use lime zest and juice instead of that of an orange.

> 1 lemon
> 1 navel orange
> 3 tablespoons extra-virgin olive oil
> 1 garlic clove, minced
> ¼ teaspoon freshly ground black pepper
> ⅛ teaspoon red pepper flakes
> 30 medium shrimp, peeled and deveined
>   Salt

Cut the zest from the whole lemon, then peel and chop half of the fruit. Cut the zest from half of the orange, then peel and chop half of the fruit. Place lemon and orange zests and chopped fruits in a medium bowl. Add oil, garlic, black pepper, and pepper flakes; stir to combine. Add shrimp and toss to coat well. Cover and marinate for 30 minutes at room temperature or overnight in the refrigerator.

Heat a grill or grill pan over medium-high heat. Remove shrimp from marinade, allowing bits of citrus to stick. Discard marinade. Season shrimp lightly with salt; grill until shrimp is opaque and cooked through, about 3 minutes per side. Squeeze a little fresh lemon or orange juice (or a combination of both) from the remaining fruit halves over the shrimp just before serving. Serve warm or at room temperature.

Makes 10 (3-piece) servings

NUTRITION AT A GLANCE
Per serving: 60 calories, 4.5 g fat, 0.5 g saturated fat, 4 g protein, 2 g carbohydrate, 0 g fiber, 25 mg sodium

MAKE-AHEAD: Shrimp can be marinated up to 1 day in advance and grilled up to 6 hours ahead. Refrigerate grilled shrimp until ready to use; bring to room temperature before serving.

Deviled Eggs

PREP TIME: 15 minutes   **COOK TIME:** 30 minutes   **CHILL TIME:** 1 hour

A throwback to the past, this egg style is still as devilishly delicious today as it was in the 1950s and 1960s, when the special plates the little mouthfuls were served on were as much the rage as the eggs themselves. We freshen up the classic recipe with a few modern additions, like tangy capers, roasted peppers, and fresh chopped chives. Boiling the eggs for a short time and then letting them sit gives the yolks a beautiful yellow color.

10 large eggs	2 tablespoons finely chopped fresh chives
¼ cup mayonnaise	2 teaspoons grainy Dijon mustard
¼ cup finely chopped roasted red peppers (from a jar)	⅛ teaspoon salt
2 tablespoons reduced-fat sour cream	Freshly ground black pepper
2 tablespoons capers, rinsed and roughly chopped	Paprika

Place eggs in a large saucepan with cold water to cover. Partially cover pan and bring water to a full boil. Reduce heat to low, cover completely, and simmer for 5 minutes. Remove from heat and let stand, covered, for 20 minutes.

Drain eggs in a colander and then run cold water over the eggs to cool. Place eggs in the refrigerator to cool completely, about 1 hour.

When cool, peel eggs and halve lengthwise. Carefully remove yolks from eggs and place in a medium bowl. Add mayonnaise, red peppers, sour cream, capers, chives, mustard, salt, and black pepper to taste; mash with a fork until well combined. Spoon 1 tablespoon of the yolk mixture into each egg white half. Sprinkle with paprika and serve.

Makes 20 egg halves

NUTRITION AT A GLANCE

Per half: 60 calories, 4.5 g fat, 1 g saturated fat, 3 g protein, 1 g carbohydrate, 0 g fiber, 110 mg sodium

MAKE-AHEAD: Eggs can be hard-boiled up to 2 days in advance, peeled, and stored in an airtight container in the refrigerator. You can fill eggs up to 2 hours before the party; carefully cover and chill until ready to serve. Garnish with paprika just before serving.

Salmon Mousse

PREP TIME: 25 minutes   **COOK TIME:** 5 minutes   **CHILL TIME:** 12 hours or overnight

This lovely party favorite can be chilled in a decorative mold for extra flair. If you serve the mousse with crackers, it becomes a Phase 2 recipe.

1 cup nonfat or low-fat plain yogurt

½ cup cold water

1 envelope unflavored gelatin

1 (15-ounce) can pink salmon, drained

⅔ cup reduced-fat sour cream

1 (6-ounce) jar prepared horseradish, drained and squeezed dry (about ¼ cup)

3 tablespoons finely chopped red onion

1 tablespoon chopped fresh dill or ½ teaspoon dried dill, crumbled

1 tablespoon Worcestershire sauce

½ teaspoon paprika

Chopped dill for garnish (optional)

60 cucumber slices or low-sodium whole-grain crackers

Place yogurt in a paper towel–lined mesh strainer and set over a bowl. Let drain for 10 minutes.

Place water in a small saucepan, sprinkle gelatin over water, and let soften 1 minute. Heat mixture over low heat, stirring, until gelatin dissolves, about 3 minutes. Do not let boil.

Purée yogurt, gelatin mixture, salmon, sour cream, horseradish, onion, dill, Worcestershire sauce, and paprika in a food processor.

Lightly coat a 1-quart fish mold, decorative bowl, terrine, or loaf pan with cooking spray; spread mousse evenly in pan. Cover and refrigerate until set, at least 12 hours or overnight. Just before serving, run a thin knife around edges of pan and invert mousse onto a platter. Sprinkle with chopped dill, if using, and surround with cucumber slices or crackers. Serve.

Makes 20 (3-tablespoon) servings

NUTRITION AT A GLANCE

Per serving (with 3 cucumber slices): 50 calories, 2.5 g fat, 1 g saturated fat, 5 g protein, 2 g carbohydrate, 0 g fiber, 150 mg sodium

Per serving (with 3 crackers): 110 calories, 5 g fat, 1 g saturated fat, 7 g protein, 11 g carbohydrate, 2 g fiber, 170 mg sodium

MAKE-AHEAD: Mousse can be made up to 1 day ahead. Keep chilled in mold, covered with plastic wrap, until ready to serve.

Parmesan Zucchini Sticks

PREP TIME: 10 minutes   **COOK TIME:** 20 minutes

These delectable nibbles will remind guests of the fried zucchini or stuffed zucchini blossoms often found at Italian feasts. Roasted, they are more healthful and every bit as good.

- 2 medium zucchini (about 1 pound)
- 1 tablespoon extra-virgin olive oil
- ¼ teaspoon dried thyme
- ⅛ teaspoon salt
- ⅛ teaspoon freshly ground black pepper
-   Pinch of red pepper flakes
- ⅓ cup freshly grated Parmesan cheese

Heat oven to 450°F. Line a baking sheet with parchment paper or foil.

Cut zucchini lengthwise into quarters, then cut into 2-inch-long sticks. Combine zucchini, oil, thyme, salt, black pepper, and pepper flakes in a medium bowl, and toss to coat. Transfer zucchini sticks to baking sheet, with a flesh side facing down. Roast until just softened and golden, turning so other flesh side is up halfway through, about 15 minutes.

Carefully turn pieces skin side down. Sprinkle evenly with cheese and continue roasting until cheese has melted, about 2 minutes. Serve warm.

Makes 10 (3-piece) servings

NUTRITION AT A GLANCE
Per serving: 35 calories, 2.5 g fat, 0.5 g saturated fat, 2 g protein, 2 g carbohydrate, 0 g fiber, 70 mg sodium

MAKE-AHEAD: Zucchini can be cut up to 1 day ahead and refrigerated in a covered container until ready to use.

Sweet Potato-Feta Rounds

PREP TIME: 20 minutes   **COOK TIME:** 25 minutes

The sturdy texture of sweet potatoes makes them perfect for roasting and using as colorful orange "cups" for tasty fillings like this one, made with feta, garlic, and chives.

3 long, thin sweet potatoes, peeled (about 1½ pounds)

1 tablespoon plus 1 teaspoon extra-virgin olive oil

1 garlic clove, minced

4 ounces reduced-fat feta cheese, crumbled (¾ cup)

2 tablespoons chopped fresh chives

   Freshly ground black pepper

Heat oven to 450°F. Line a baking sheet with parchment paper or foil.

Cut potatoes into 30 (¾-inch-thick) rounds. With a melon baller, carefully scoop a pocket into each potato piece, being careful not to scoop through bottoms; discard scooped-out portion.

Combine potato pieces, 1 tablespoon of the oil, and garlic in a large bowl; toss to coat. Spread potatoes out on the baking sheet, scooped-out side up, and roast until potatoes are just tender and edges are starting to brown, 18 to 20 minutes.

Meanwhile, mash feta, chives, and remaining 1 teaspoon oil together in a small bowl. Season with pepper to taste.

Remove potatoes from oven and fill each pocket with a heaping ½ teaspoon cheese mixture. Return to oven and bake until heated through, about 5 minutes. Serve warm.

Makes 10 (3-piece) servings

NUTRITION AT A GLANCE

Per serving: 80 calories, 2.5 g fat, 1 g saturated fat, 3 g protein, 11 g carbohydrate, 2 g fiber, 150 mg sodium

MAKE-AHEAD: Cheese mixture can be prepared up to 1 day ahead; refrigerate in a covered container until ready to use. Sweet potatoes can be roasted (without cheese mixture) up to 8 hours before the party; cover and leave at room temperature. Fill with cheese mixture and warm through just before serving.

Chocolate-Dipped Strawberries

PREP TIME: 10 minutes   **COOK TIME:** 10 minutes   **CHILL TIME:** 15 minutes

Toasted sesame seeds add extra crunch and a tasty surprise to this easy-to-eat dessert. Look for large strawberries with stems for the nicest presentation.

⅓ cup walnut pieces, finely chopped

2 tablespoons sesame seeds

3 ounces bittersweet chocolate

2 tablespoons fat-free half-and-half

20 large strawberries with stems (about 2 pints), rinsed and dried

Heat oven to 275°F. Spread walnuts on a baking sheet and bake until fragrant and lightly browned, about 10 minutes.

While nuts are toasting, place sesame seeds in a small skillet over medium-low heat. Cook, gently shaking pan back and forth, until seeds are golden, about 5 minutes. Allow nuts and seeds to cool, then mix together in a shallow bowl.

Heat chocolate and half-and-half in a small saucepan over medium-low heat, whisking until chocolate is melted, about 3 minutes.

Line a baking pan with wax paper.

Dip strawberries into chocolate (about three-quarters of the way in), then dip one side into nut and seed mixture, coating well. Place nut side up in baking pan. Refrigerate until chocolate is set, about 15 minutes, and serve.

Makes 10 (2-piece) servings

NUTRITION AT A GLANCE
Per serving: 90 calories, 7 g fat, 2 g saturated fat, 2 g protein, 8 g carbohydrate, 2 g fiber, 0 mg sodium

MAKE-AHEAD: Walnuts and sesame seeds can be toasted up to 3 days ahead. Strawberries can be dipped up to 8 hours ahead. Carefully cover berries and refrigerate; do not freeze.

Cannoli Tartlets

PREP TIME: 10 minutes   **CHILL TIME:** 2 hours

A classic Italian favorite, cannoli gets a light update here that's as sweet as ever. You can find prebaked mini whole-wheat phyllo shells in the refrigerator section of most supermarkets.

- 2 cups part-skim ricotta cheese
- ¼ cup granular sugar substitute
- 4 ounces bittersweet chocolate, finely chopped
  Pinch of ground cinnamon
- 1 teaspoon vanilla extract
- 2 boxes mini whole-wheat phyllo shells (15 shells each)
- ¼ cup finely chopped unsalted pistachio nuts

Stir together ricotta, sugar substitute, chocolate, cinnamon, and vanilla in a medium bowl until well combined. Chill, covered, until ready to prepare tartlets.

No more than 2 hours before serving, fill mini phyllo shells with about 1 tablespoon ricotta filling. Sprinkle each tartlet evenly with pistachios and refrigerate until ready to serve.

Makes 30 tartlets

NUTRITION AT A GLANCE
Per tartlet: 70 calories, 4.5 g fat, 1.5 g saturated fat, 3 g protein, 5 g carbohydrate, 0 g fiber, 30 mg sodium

MAKE-AHEAD: The ricotta filling can be made up to 1 day in advance and refrigerated in a covered container. Tartlets can be filled up to 2 hours ahead of serving and refrigerated, lightly covered, until ready to serve.

Raspberry-Ginger Fizzes

PREP TIME: 5 minutes

The vibrant red color and sprightly flavor of this fresh-tasting fruit and ginger drink will make homemade soda fans of all your friends.

- 1 (10-ounce) package frozen raspberries, thawed, with juices
- 1 (¾-inch) piece fresh ginger, peeled
- 2 tablespoons granular sugar substitute
- 1 (2-liter) bottle seltzer water, chilled
- Ice cubes (optional)

To make the drink base: Purée raspberries and their juices, ginger, and sugar substitute in a blender. Strain the mixture through a fine-mesh sieve. For each drink, place 4½ teaspoons of the base in an 8-ounce glass. Add ¾ cup seltzer and stir rapidly. Add a few ice cubes, if desired, and stir again. Serve.

Makes 10 (¾-cup) drinks

NUTRITION AT A GLANCE
Per drink: 60 calories, 4.5 g fat, 0.5 g saturated fat, 4 g protein, 2 g carbohydrate, 0 g fiber, 25 mg sodium

MAKE-AHEAD: Raspberry-ginger drink base can be made up to 1 day ahead and refrigerated in a covered container until ready to use. Add seltzer water to drinks individually, just before serving.

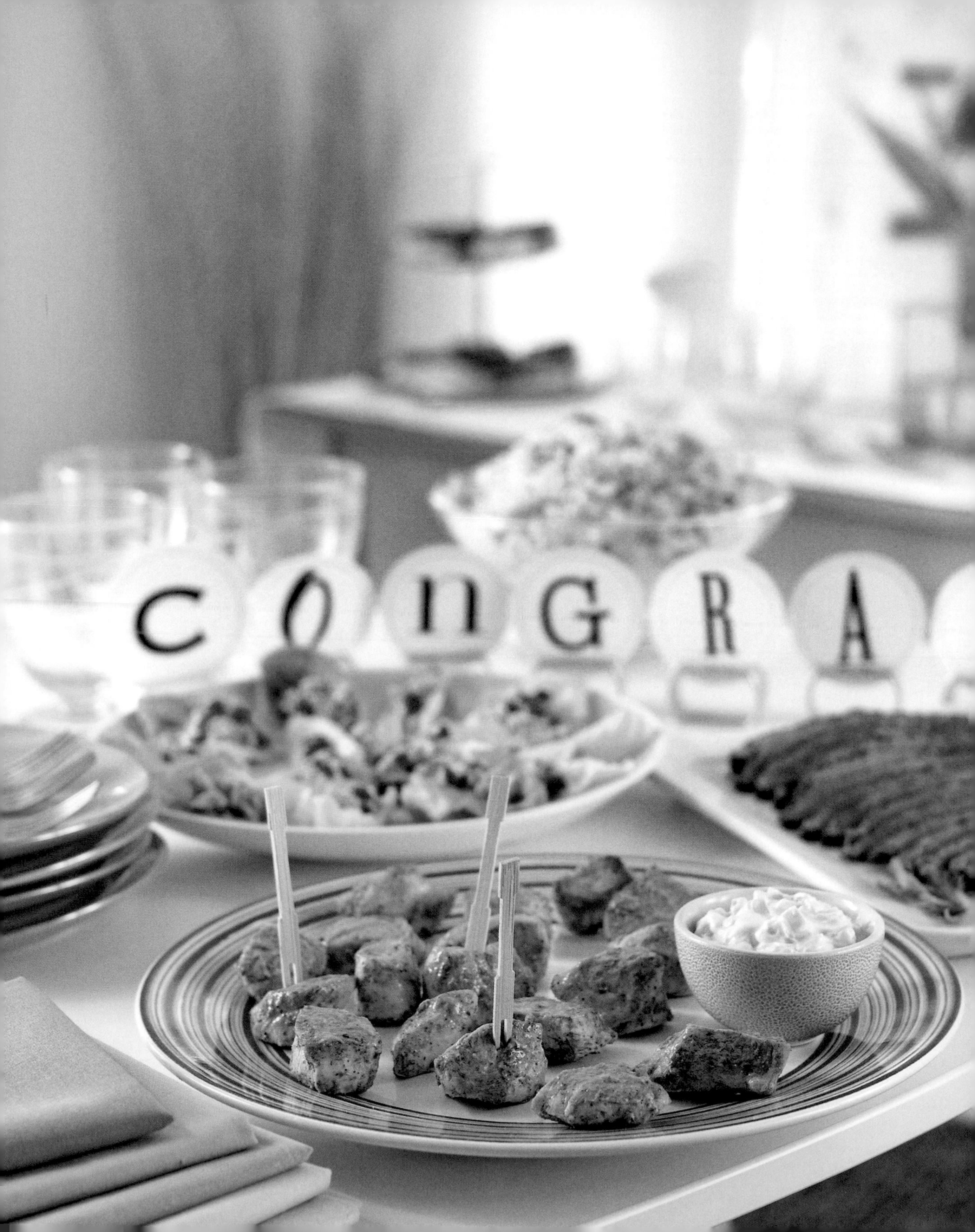
CONGRA

RITE OF PASSAGE PARTY

FOR 8 GUESTS

Big birthdays, milestone anniversaries, graduations, engagements, confirmations, job promotions, and more—there are all sorts of occasions worth celebrating in honor of our growth or good fortune. At this party, you'll serve an array of crowd-pleasing dishes that fall right in line with your South Beach Diet lifestyle. Juicy flank steak spiced with cayenne and cumin is both hearty and lean; fiber-rich brown rice is seasoned with sweet grilled onions and herbs; and a nutrient-rich slaw is filled with a lively mix of colorful cabbages and snow peas. All these dishes work indoors or out and taste just as great at room temperature as they do warm.

The guest of honor is the focus of this party, and from the invitations to the party itself, you'll want to incorporate personal touches that will make that person feel extra special. Ask guests to jot down some great moments they've shared with the honoree, then set aside a little time for these fond memories to be read aloud.

◀ *Congratulations will extend to the cook for providing the great food at this celebratory meal.*

MENU

Curried Chicken Skewers with Yogurt Dip

Italian Tuna Salad Bites

Spicy Flank Steak

Brown Rice with Grilled Red Onions, Lemon, and Thyme

Festive 5-Veggie Slaw

Sponge Cake with Chocolate Sour Cream Frosting

Party Game Plan

Up to 1 month before: Make and freeze brown rice.

Up to 1 week before: Make spice mix for steak.

Up to 2 days before: Make yogurt dip; marinate steak.

Up to 1 day before: Prepare tuna; make dressing for slaw; thaw rice.

Day of: Make cake; bake chicken; dress slaw; assemble tuna bites; finish rice; grill steak.

Curried Chicken Skewers with Yogurt Dip

PREP TIME: 25 minutes   **COOK TIME:** 15 minutes

Tangy and creamy, yogurt not only helps the spices and flavorings adhere to the chicken but is the basis for the dip as well. Use a garlic press, if you have one, for both the garlic and the ginger, so that they release their essential oils.

Yogurt Dip

- ½ cup nonfat or low-fat plain yogurt
- ½ celery stalk, minced
- 2 teaspoons fresh lime juice
- ⅛ teaspoon salt
- Freshly ground black pepper

Chicken

- 3 tablespoons nonfat or low-fat plain yogurt
- 1 tablespoon curry powder
- 1 teaspoon minced fresh ginger
- 1 small garlic clove, minced
- 3 (6-ounce) boneless, skinless chicken breasts, cut into 32 (¾-inch) cubes
- Salt and freshly ground black pepper
- 1 tablespoon canola oil

Heat oven to 400°F.

For the yogurt dip: Combine yogurt, celery, lime juice, salt, and pepper to taste in a small bowl; set aside.

For the chicken: Combine yogurt, curry powder, ginger, and garlic in a large bowl; set aside.

Season chicken lightly with salt and pepper. Heat oil in a large nonstick skillet over medium-high heat. Add chicken and cook until browned on all sides, 5 minutes. Transfer chicken pieces to yogurt–curry mixture and toss to coat.

Place chicken in a single layer in a large baking pan; bake for 10 minutes. Skewer each cube of chicken with a toothpick and serve warm with yogurt dip.

Makes 8 (4-skewer) servings and ⅔ cup dip

NUTRITION AT A GLANCE

Per serving (with 1 generous tablespoon dip): 100 calories, 2.5 g fat, 0 g saturated fat, 16 g protein, 3 g carbohydrate, 0 g fiber, 95 mg sodium

MAKE-AHEAD: Dip can be made up to 2 days in advance and refrigerated in a covered container until ready to use. Bring to room temperature before serving.

Italian Tuna Salad Bites

PREP TIME: 20 minutes

This recipe calls for canned tuna, which is easy and convenient. But it can also be prepared with fresh grilled tuna when you want to make an extra-special dish. Just substitute an equal amount of fresh tuna for the canned. If the sun-dried tomatoes aren't particularly dry, there's no need to soak them.

2　sun-dried tomatoes

1　(6-ounce) can water-packed chunk light tuna, drained and flaked

2　teaspoons extra-virgin olive oil

1　teaspoon red wine vinegar

⅛　teaspoon dried oregano

⅛　teaspoon salt

　　Freshly ground black pepper

6　inner romaine leaves, cut into 24 (1½-inch) pieces

If needed, cover tomatoes with warm water and soak for 15 minutes to soften. Drain and mince.

　　Combine tomatoes, tuna, oil, vinegar, oregano, salt, and pepper to taste in a small bowl. Spoon 1 teaspoon of the tuna mixture onto each romaine piece. Arrange on a platter and serve.

Makes 8 (3-piece) servings

NUTRITION AT A GLANCE

Per serving: 45 calories, 1 g fat, 0 g saturated fat, 6 g protein, 3 g carbohydrate, 0 g fiber, 195 mg sodium

MAKE-AHEAD: Tuna mixture can be made 1 day in advance and stored in a covered container in the refrigerator until ready to use. Place on romaine leaves just before serving.

Spicy Flank Steak

PREP TIME: 5 minutes   **MARINATING TIME:** 30 minutes or overnight   **COOK TIME:** 10 minutes

A few dried spices and herbs is all it takes to make a fantastic rub for meat or chicken. You can add more or less of any of the spices, if you wish. This rub works well with flank, loin, and round steak cuts, all of which are lean and flavorful.

2	(1½-pound) flank steaks, about 1 inch thick
¼	cup extra-virgin olive oil
1	tablespoon plus 1 teaspoon paprika
1	teaspoon ground coriander
1	teaspoon ground cumin
1	teaspoon dried oregano
¼	teaspoon cayenne pepper
¼	teaspoon salt
⅛	teaspoon freshly ground black pepper

Place steaks in a 9- by 13-inch glass baking dish.

Whisk together oil, paprika, coriander, cumin, oregano, cayenne, salt, and black pepper in a small bowl; pour marinade over steaks. Marinate steaks for 30 minutes at room temperature or overnight in the refrigerator, turning once or twice.

Heat a grill or grill pan to medium-high. Grill steaks 4 to 5 minutes per side for medium-rare. Discard remaining marinade. Allow steaks to rest 5 minutes before cutting into thin slices against the grain. Serve warm.

Makes 8 (6-ounce) servings

NUTRITION AT A GLANCE
Per serving: 350 calories, 21 g fat, 7 g saturated fat, 36 g protein, 1 g carbohydrate, 0 g fiber, 170 mg sodium

MAKE-AHEAD: Steak can be marinated for up to 2 days; bring to room temperature before grilling. Spice mix can be prepared up to 1 week in advance and stored in a covered container in your pantry.

Brown Rice with Grilled Red Onions, Lemon, and Thyme

PREP TIME: 10 minutes   **COOK TIME:** 45 minutes

Mixing brown rice with grilled vegetables, herbs, and citrus makes a healthy and very tasty side dish that can be endlessly modified. Try grilled tomatoes and zucchini with fresh basil, for example, or any other combination you like.

2½	cups water
1¼	cups brown rice
1	teaspoon dried thyme
1	large red onion, cut into ¼-inch-thick slices
2	tablespoons extra-virgin olive oil
	Salt and freshly ground black pepper
1	tablespoon fresh lemon juice

Bring water to a boil in a medium saucepan; stir in rice and thyme. Cover pan, reduce heat to low, and simmer until rice is tender and water is absorbed, about 40 minutes.

Meanwhile, heat a grill or grill pan to medium-high. Brush onion slices with 1 tablespoon of the oil and season lightly with salt and pepper. Grill onions until softened and lightly charred, 3 to 5 minutes per side. Cool briefly, then chop onions into small pieces.

When rice is cooked, fluff with a fork and transfer to a serving bowl. Stir in onions. Add remaining 1 tablespoon oil and lemon juice, adjust seasonings, and serve warm.

Makes 8 (generous ½-cup) servings

NUTRITION AT A GLANCE
Per serving: 150 calories, 4.5 g fat, 0.5 g saturated fat, 2 g protein, 27 g carbohydrate, 2 g fiber, 75 mg sodium

MAKE-AHEAD: Brown rice can be cooked, cooled, and refrigerated a covered container up to 2 days in advance, or it can be frozen for up to 1 month. Reheat in a microwave or covered in a warm oven before tossing with the other ingredients.

Festive 5-Veggie Slaw

PREP TIME: 20 minutes   **MARINATING TIME:** 1 hour or overnight

Far from just shredded cabbage, this slaw resembles confetti with its vibrant colors. Its flavor is definitely something to celebrate.

1	(2½- to 3-pound) head Napa cabbage, shredded (4 cups)
1	(1-pound) head red cabbage, shredded (4 cups)
2	ounces spinach leaves, shredded (1½ cups)
18	snow peas, thinly sliced on the diagonal
3	scallions, thinly sliced on the diagonal
1	tablespoon plus 1½ teaspoons red wine vinegar
1½	teaspoons Dijon mustard
¼	cup extra-virgin olive oil
	Salt and freshly ground black pepper

Combine Napa and red cabbages, spinach, snow peas, and scallions in a large bowl.

Whisk together vinegar and mustard in a small bowl; slowly whisk in oil. Pour dressing over vegetables and toss to coat; season to taste with salt and pepper. Let slaw marinate for at least 1 hour in the refrigerator. Bring to room temperature before serving.

Makes 8 (1-cup) servings

NUTRITION AT A GLANCE
Per serving: 90 calories, 7 g fat, 1 g saturated fat, 2 g protein, 6 g carbohydrate, 2 g fiber, 30 mg sodium

MAKE-AHEAD: Dressing can be made up to 1 day ahead and stored in a covered container in the refrigerator. Slaw can be assembled up to 8 hours in advance and refrigerated in a covered container; bring to room temperature before serving.

Sponge Cake with Chocolate Sour Cream Frosting

PREP TIME: 15 minutes   **COOK TIME:** 30 minutes

This light-textured sponge cake becomes a rich indulgence when topped with a creamy, chocolaty frosting.

Cake

- ¾ cup whole-grain pastry flour
- ½ cup white pastry flour
- ½ teaspoon baking powder
- 6 eggs, separated
- ¾ teaspoon cream of tartar
- ¾ cup granular sugar substitute
- ⅓ cup unsweetened applesauce
- ½ cup fat-free milk
- 1 teaspoon vanilla extract
- ¼ teaspoon salt

Frosting

- 1 cup reduced-fat sour cream
- 1 cup bittersweet chocolate chips
- 2 tablespoons granular sugar substitute
- 1 teaspoon vanilla extract

Heat oven to 325°F. Lightly coat a 9- by 13-inch baking pan with cooking spray.

For the cake: Sift whole-grain and white flours and baking powder into a medium bowl.

In a large bowl, with an electric mixer at high speed, beat egg whites until frothy, about 1 minute. Add cream of tartar and continue beating on high until stiff peaks form, 2 to 3 minutes. Gradually add ½ cup of the sugar substitute and beat until you have a smooth, glossy meringue, about 30 seconds more. Set aside.

In another large bowl, using same beaters, beat egg yolks on high speed for 2 minutes. Add remaining ¼ cup sugar substitute, applesauce, milk, vanilla, and salt; continue beating until mixture is light, airy, and smooth, about 1 minute more. Fold flour mixture into egg yolk mixture just until combined.

Add flour mixture to meringue and gently fold until whites are nearly incorporated. Pour into prepared pan and bake until cake springs back when lightly touched and a tester inserted into center comes out clean, 22 to 25 minutes. Cool in pan on a wire rack.

For the frosting: When cake is cool, combine sour cream and chocolate chips in a small saucepan. Cook over low heat, stirring constantly, until chips are melted and frosting is smooth, about 3 minutes. Add sugar substitute and cook, stirring, until dissolved, about 30 seconds more. Stir in vanilla.

Spread warm frosting over cake and let cool at room temperature until frosting sets, about 1 hour. Cake can remain at room temperature for up to 4 hours.

Makes 12 servings

NUTRITION AT A GLANCE
Per serving: 190 calories, 9 g fat, 4.5 g saturated fat, 6 g protein, 22 g carbohydrate, 1 g fiber, 120 mg sodium

MAKE-AHEAD: Sponge cake can be baked and frosted up to 4 hours ahead. Cover lightly and let sit at room temperature until ready to serve.

TIP **Beating egg whites:** Eggs separate most easily when cold. However, when beating whites for a recipe, let them come to room temperature first; you get more volume this way. Adding a bit of cream of tartar to the whites helps them reach their full volume; a little lemon juice or vinegar achieves the same thing. Use beaten egg whites immediately; they will lose their volume as they sit.

HOLIDAYS

New Year's Day Open House

Valentine's Day Dinner for 2

Passover Seder

Easter Gathering

Cinco de Mayo Celebration

Mother's Day Luncheon

Fourth of July Revel

Thanksgiving

Hanukkah Party

Christmas Eve Dinner

Christmas Day

NEW YEAR'S DAY OPEN HOUSE

FOR 12 GUESTS

A New Year's Day open house is a naturally social affair and a great way to reconnect with friends after the rush of the holiday season. You'll prepare most of this menu in advance, ensuring plenty of mingle and chat time throughout the day. Light yet satisfying, most of the dishes are Phase 1, offering a nice change of pace after the holidays.

Open-house parties tend to last about 4 hours. Invite guests for 1 P.M. and plan on entertaining until 5. Since friends will come and go as they please, you'll want to make sure to have enough food for latecomers to eat. Set out half when the first guests arrive, then more as others show up. Cut all of the salmon roulades ahead so they're ready to go straight to your serving plate when needed. Dress just half the salad, until you need the rest. And keep the cooked cioppino in the pot so that it can easily be reheated to serve as the second wave of New Year's celebrants rolls in.

◄ *The best way to ring in the New Year is with good food and good friends. This help-yourself menu perfectly suits the open-house format.*

MENU

Smoked Salmon Roulades

Braised Mini Meatballs

Green Salad with Mushrooms and Sunflower Seeds

Cioppino

Hoppin' John Salad

Savory Cheddar Cheese Biscuits

Mocha-Hazelnut Brownies

Pomegranate Punch

Holiday Game Plan

Up to 1 month before: Make and freeze biscuits and brownies.

Up to 2 weeks before: Make and freeze meatballs and tomato sauce for cioppino.

Up to 1 day before: Make roulades (but do not slice); thaw biscuits, brownies, and meatballs; make hoppin' John; prepare salad dressing.

Day of: Finish cioppino; slice roulades; assemble and dress salad; warm biscuits, meatballs, and hoppin' John; make punch.

Smoked Salmon Roulades

PREP TIME: 15 minutes   **CHILL TIME:** 15 minutes

Making roulades is easier than you might think and yields impressive results that lend an extra-special touch. Like its fresh counterpart, smoked salmon provides ample nutrients, including B vitamins and omega-3 essential fatty acids.

- 8 ounces sliced smoked salmon
- 4 ounces fat-free cream cheese, softened at room temperature
- 2 tablespoons capers, rinsed and chopped
- ½ teaspoon grated lemon zest
    Freshly ground black pepper

Place a 16-inch sheet of plastic wrap on a clean work surface. Arrange salmon slices, overlapping slightly, to make a 9- by 13-inch rectangle. Trim the edges, if necessary, to make an even rectangle.

Stir cream cheese in a small bowl to further soften it and make spreading easier. Carefully spread cream cheese over salmon, leaving a ¼-inch border on each of the long sides. Sprinkle capers and zest evenly over salmon, then sprinkle lightly with pepper.

Using the plastic wrap to help, lift one long end of salmon and roll it over (without the plastic) until you have a 13-inch-long cylinder. Wrap the cylinder tightly in plastic wrap and place in the freezer for 15 minutes, until firm.

Slice salmon crosswise into 24 (½-inch-thick) slices. Serve each slice on its side to achieve the pinwheel effect.

Makes 24 pieces

NUTRITION AT A GLANCE
Per piece: 15 calories, 0 g fat, 0 g saturated fat, 2 g protein, 0 g carbohydrate, 0 g fiber, 240 mg sodium

MAKE-AHEAD: Roulades can be made up to 1 day in advance; wrap the cylinder in plastic wrap and refrigerate (forgo the freezer step if making ahead). You can slice up to 8 hours before serving and keep chilled and covered until ready to serve.

Braised Mini Meatballs

PREP TIME: 15 minutes   **COOK TIME:** 55 minutes

If this is your first time making meatballs without breadcrumbs, be prepared for a terrific surprise. Not only do these scrumptious minis hold together beautifully, they are just as delightful as those made with bread. To prevent the meatball mixture from sticking to your hands while forming the balls, simply dampen your hands first.

1½ pounds extra-lean ground beef	¼ teaspoon salt
2 large eggs	2 teaspoons extra-virgin olive oil
1 medium onion, finely chopped	1 cup dry red wine
½ cup chopped fresh parsley, plus more for garnish	¼ cup unsalted tomato paste
1 teaspoon dried basil	2 cups lower-sodium beef broth
¾ teaspoon freshly ground black pepper	2 teaspoons granular sugar substitute

Combine beef, eggs, onion, parsley, basil, pepper, and salt in a large bowl. Mix well with wet hands or a wooden spoon. Form into 36 (1¼-inch) meatballs.

Heat oil over medium-high heat in a large nonstick skillet. Carefully add meatballs to the skillet (this can be done in batches, if necessary) and cook until browned on all sides, 5 to 7 minutes per batch. Pour off any excess fat from the skillet. Return all meatballs to the skillet and reduce heat to low.

Whisk together wine and tomato paste in a small bowl; pour over meatballs. Simmer over low heat, stirring occasionally, until tomato mixture has thickened, about 10 minutes. Add broth and simmer until sauce is slightly thickened, about 30 minutes. Stir in sugar substitute. Sprinkle with additional parsley just before serving. Serve warm or at room temperature.

Makes 12 (3-piece) servings

NUTRITION AT A GLANCE
Per serving: 120 calories, 4.5 g fat, 1.5 g saturated fat, 15 g protein, 3 g carbohydrate, 0 g fiber, 132 mg sodium

MAKE-AHEAD: Meatballs can be cooked, cooled, and frozen for up to 2 weeks. Defrost in the refrigerator before gently heating on the stove top over low heat.

Green Salad with Mushrooms and Sunflower Seeds

PREP TIME: 15 minutes

This large salad provides a refreshing counterpoint to the rich dishes in this menu. Sunflower seeds add an unexpected crunch as well as good amounts of the antioxidant vitamin E.

1	(½-pound) head green leaf lettuce, torn into bite-size pieces (about 8 cups)
½	pound spinach, torn into bite-size pieces (about 8 cups)
½	pound white mushrooms, thinly sliced
½	cup roasted unsalted sunflower seeds
2½	tablespoons sherry vinegar
1½	teaspoons Dijon mustard
⅓	cup extra-virgin olive oil
1	tablespoon warm water
	Salt and freshly ground black pepper

Combine lettuce, spinach, mushrooms, and sunflower seeds in a large serving bowl; set aside.

Whisk together vinegar and mustard in a medium bowl until smooth. Slowly whisk in oil until completely incorporated, then whisk in the warm water. Toss salad with dressing just before serving and season to taste with salt and pepper.

Makes 12 (1½-cup) servings

NUTRITION AT A GLANCE
Per serving: 110 calories, 10 g fat, 1.5 g saturated fat, 3 g protein, 4 g carbohydrate, 2 g fiber, 85 mg sodium

MAKE-AHEAD: Dressing can be made up to 1 day in advance; bring to room temperature and whisk well before using.

Cioppino

PREP TIME: 25 minutes   **COOK TIME:** 1 hour

Said to have originated with Italian immigrants in the San Francisco Bay area, this hearty, spicy shellfish stew is as satisfying and sumptuous as it is simple to make.

1 tablespoon extra-virgin olive oil

2 medium onions, chopped

3 garlic cloves, minced

1 bay leaf

1 teaspoon dried oregano

½ teaspoon red pepper flakes

1 large green bell pepper, chopped

1 cup dry red wine

2 tablespoons tomato paste

2 (28-ounce) cans unsalted chopped tomatoes

1 cup water

2 (6.5-ounce) cans chopped clams, with juices

Salt and freshly ground black pepper

1 pound mussels, scrubbed and debearded

1 pound firm-fleshed white fish (such as hake or cod), cut into 1-inch chunks

1 pound large shrimp, peeled and deveined, with tails left intact

3 tablespoons chopped fresh basil

Heat oil in a large nonstick saucepan over medium heat. Add onions, garlic, bay leaf, oregano, and pepper flakes; cook until onions have softened, about 5 minutes. Stir in bell pepper and cook 1 minute more.

Whisk together wine and tomato paste in a small bowl; add to onion mixture. Simmer until reduced by half, about 5 minutes. Add tomatoes and water; cover and simmer for 30 minutes.

Stir in clams and their juices. Season to taste with salt and pepper. Add mussels, cover pan, and simmer 5 minutes. Add fish and shrimp; simmer until fish is cooked through, about 5 minutes more. Discard any unopened mussels. Stir in basil just before serving.

Makes 12 (1-cup) servings

NUTRITION AT A GLANCE

Per serving: 190 calories, 3 g fat, 0.5 g saturated fat, 23 g protein, 13 g carbohydrate, 3 g fiber, 270 mg sodium

MAKE-AHEAD: Tomato sauce can be made up to 2 days in advance and refrigerated in a covered container until ready to use; or it can be frozen for up to 2 weeks. Just before serving, bring the sauce to a simmer and proceed with the recipe by adding the canned clams and fresh fish and shellfish.

Hoppin' John Salad

PREP TIME: 15 minutes   **COOK TIME:** 15 minutes

Though historians can't officially explain the name of this traditional Southern dish, folklore suggests it may refer to a children's custom of hopping around the table whenever it was served. Tasty black-eyed peas are on the table throughout the South on New Year's Day for good luck. Serve hot pepper sauce on the side for those who like extra spice.

½ pound lower-fat, lower-sodium smoked ham
   (not honey glazed), in one piece (about ½ inch thick)

1 tablespoon canola oil

2 medium onions, chopped

4 celery stalks, diced

1 large green bell pepper, chopped

2 (15.5-ounce) cans black-eyed peas, rinsed and drained

¼ teaspoon hot pepper sauce

⅓ cup chopped fresh parsley

   Freshly ground black pepper

Cut ham into ½-inch cubes. Heat oil in a large nonstick skillet over medium heat. Add onions, celery, and green pepper; cook until softened, 8 to 10 minutes. Stir in ham, black-eyed peas, and hot pepper sauce; cook until heated through, about 5 minutes more. Stir in parsley just before serving and season to taste with black pepper. Serve warm or at room temperature.

Makes 12 (½-cup) servings

NUTRITION AT A GLANCE

Per serving: 90 calories, 2.5 g fat, 0.5 g saturated fat, 7 g protein, 10 g carbohydrate, 2 g fiber, 360 mg sodium

MAKE-AHEAD: Recipe can be made 1 day ahead and kept covered in the refrigerator. Gently warm before serving or serve at room temperature.

Savory Cheddar Cheese Biscuits

PREP TIME: 15 minutes   **COOK TIME:** 20 minutes

These drop biscuits puff up light, airy, and full of cheesy flavor. The recipe lends itself well to variations: Try adding minced jalapeño, minced garlic, a different reduced-fat cheese (such as feta or goat), or other herbs (such as rosemary or basil).

2½ cups whole-grain pastry flour

1 tablespoon baking powder

¼ teaspoon baking soda

1½ teaspoons dried thyme

½ teaspoon freshly ground black pepper

¼ teaspoon salt

¼ cup plus 2 tablespoons chilled trans-fat-free margarine, cut into bits

12 ounces reduced-fat cheddar cheese, shredded (3 cups)

1⅓ cups fat-free milk

Heat oven to 400°F. Lightly coat 2 baking sheets with cooking spray.

Whisk together flour, baking powder, baking soda, thyme, pepper, and salt in a large bowl. Add margarine and, using a pastry cutter or 2 knives, blend until mixture resembles coarse meal. Add cheese and toss to coat. Slowly stir in milk and mix just to combine.

Drop dough by ¼ cupfuls onto baking sheet, about 2 inches apart. Bake until edges and tops are golden, 14 to 16 minutes. Serve warm or at room temperature.

Makes 20 biscuits

NUTRITION AT A GLANCE
Per biscuit: 140 calories, 7 g fat, 3.5 g saturated fat, 7 g protein, 14 g carbohydrate, 2 g fiber, 150 mg sodium

MAKE-AHEAD: Biscuits can be frozen for up to 1 month. Defrost and bring to room temperature before heating in a warm oven. If you don't freeze the biscuits first, you can freeze any leftovers.

Mocha-Hazelnut Brownies

PREP TIME: 10 minutes   **COOK TIME:** 30 minutes

These decadent, chocolaty squares are delicate, so use a small spatula to transfer them from the pan to a serving platter.

¾ cup hazelnuts, skinned	½ cup trans-fat-free margarine
2 ounces bittersweet chocolate	1 tablespoon vanilla extract
½ cup whole-grain pastry flour	¼ cup granular sugar substitute
½ teaspoon ground cinnamon	2 large eggs
1½ teaspoons instant coffee powder	½ cup bittersweet chocolate chips, roughly chopped

Heat oven to 350°F. Lightly coat an 8- by 8-inch baking pan with cooking spray.

Place hazelnuts on a baking sheet and toast until fragrant and lightly golden, 8 to 10 minutes. Cool briefly, then roughly chop.

Heat chocolate in a small saucepan over medium-low heat, whisking constantly, until melted, about 1 minute. Remove from heat and let cool to room temperature.

Sift flour, cinnamon, and coffee powder into a medium bowl; set aside.

In a large bowl, with an electric mixer at high speed, beat margarine and vanilla until creamy. Add sugar substitute and continue to beat on high until well mixed. Add eggs, 1 at a time, scraping down the sides of the bowl with a rubber spatula, and beat to combine. Add melted chocolate and beat until combined. Stir in hazelnuts and chocolate chips.

Pour batter into the baking pan and bake until a tester inserted in the center comes out clean, about 20 minutes. Cool completely, cut into 32 (1- by 2-inch) pieces, and serve.

Makes 32 brownies

NUTRITION AT A GLANCE
Per brownie: 70 calories, 6 g fat, 1.5 g saturated fat, 1 g protein, 5 g carbohydrate, 0 g fiber, 30 mg sodium

MAKE-AHEAD: Brownies can be made 1 day ahead and stored in an airtight container at room temperature or in the refrigerator. Or they can be frozen for up to 1 month.

Pomegranate Punch

PREP TIME: 5 minutes

Celebrating New Year's with a chilled, bubbly pink drink is nothing short of apropos. This nonalcoholic punch is pretty and filled with all sorts of healthy goodness from the pomegranate juice. Make the punch in a pitcher, then pour over ice, so that the bubbles stay lively.

1	orange, unpeeled
1	lemon, unpeeled
1	(2-liter) bottle seltzer water, chilled
1½	cups unsweetened 100% pomegranate juice

Cut 4 thin slices each from orange and lemon, then quarter slices. Combine seltzer, pomegranate juice, and orange and lemon quarters in a pitcher. Pour over ice and serve.

Makes 20 (½-cup) drinks

NUTRITION AT A GLANCE
Per drink: 20 calories, 0 g fat, 0 g saturated fat, 0 g protein, 5 g carbohydrate, 0 g fiber, 0 mg sodium

TIP **About pomegranate juice:** A wonderful combination of slightly sweet and slightly tart flavors, pomegranate juice packs a punch when it comes to nutrients (it's a great source of vitamins A, C, and E). You can purchase 100% pomegranate juice in your local health-food store or in the health-food section of your grocery store. Stay away from pomegranate juice "cocktail" products, which are generally high in sugar. Remember, you can enjoy pomegranate seeds (which offer plenty of fiber) on Phase 2, but wait to enjoy the juice until Phase 3 since it's quite caloric.

VALENTINE'S DAY DINNER FOR 2

FOR 2 GUESTS

Why go out for an expensive dinner on Valentine's Day when you can woo your sweetie with a romantic home-cooked meal? From crisp cucumber cups filled with a fresh shrimp and artichoke salad to juicy, balsamic-glazed steak, ruby Swiss chard, and a stack of sliced tomatoes baked with feta cheese and herbs, you're certain to please with this delectable, heart-warming fare.

To cleanse the palate after the main course, serve a refreshing grapefruit and avocado salad sprinkled with pistachio nuts. And for dessert, offer a beautiful strawberry blancmange chilled in heart-shaped molds. Flutes of very dry sparkling rosé make the perfect accompaniment.

Other special touches can include candles and flowers, but be sure to keep the centerpiece low so it doesn't obstruct your view of each other. And remember that this elegant dinner doesn't have to center around romance. It's also perfect when shared with a parent or a great friend.

◀ *Your special guest will love the fitting red theme of this Valentine's Day dinner. Setting a beautiful table shows just how much you care.*

MENU

*Shrimp Salad in
Cucumber Cups*

Balsamic-Glazed Sirloin Steak

Ruby Swiss Chard Sauté

*Baked Tomatoes with
Feta and Herbs*

Grapefruit and Avocado Salad

Strawberry Blancmange

Holiday Game Plan

Up to 3 days before: Toast pistachios for grapefruit salad.

Up to 1 day before: Marinate steak; make blancmange.

Day of: Prepare chard; make shrimp salad and fill cucumber cups; cook chard; bake tomatoes; assemble salad; grill steak.

Shrimp Salad in Cucumber Cups

PREP TIME: 15 minutes   **COOK TIME:** 5 minutes

Light and elegant, this simple starter is sure to impress your special dining partner. The flavorful liquid from the artichoke hearts is the secret ingredient here.

1¼ cups water	4 marinated artichoke heart quarters, roughly chopped, plus 1 teaspoon of the liquid
10 whole peppercorns	
1 (¼-inch-thick) lemon slice	1 tablespoon fresh lemon juice
1 bay leaf	1 tablespoon chopped fresh basil
8 medium shrimp, peeled and deveined	2 medium (8-inch) cucumbers

Bring water, peppercorns, lemon slice, and bay leaf to a simmer in a small saucepan over medium-high heat; simmer for 1 minute. Add shrimp, cover pan, and remove pan from heat. Let shrimp sit in poaching liquid until opaque and cooked through, 3 to 4 minutes. Transfer shrimp to a cutting board and roughly chop.

Place shrimp in a medium bowl; add artichoke hearts and the 1 teaspoon liquid, lemon juice, and basil; stir to combine.

Using a sharp knife, trim ends of cucumbers. Cut each cucumber crosswise into 4 pieces, each about 2 inches long. Cut straight sides down each piece to square it, leaving the peel intact just at the corners.

Using a melon baller, cut a small cup, about 1 inch deep, into each cucumber piece. Fill each cup with 2 tablespoons of shrimp mixture and serve.

Makes 2 (4-piece) servings

NUTRITION AT A GLANCE
Per serving: 80 calories, 2.5 g fat, 0 g saturated fat, 7 g protein, 9 g carbohydrate, 3 g fiber, 160 mg sodium

MAKE-AHEAD: Cucumbers can be cut, wrapped in plastic wrap, and refrigerated up to 8 hours in advance. Shrimp mixture can also be prepared up to 8 hours ahead and refrigerated in a covered container; bring to room temperature and fill cups just before serving.

Balsamic-Glazed Sirloin Steak

PREP TIME: 5 minutes   **MARINATING TIME:** 4 hours or overnight   **COOK TIME:** 10 minutes

Marinating the meat for at least 4 hours, or better yet overnight, then basting it with the marinade while cooking doubles the flavor and makes this tender, juicy steak special. If you don't have a grill pan, use a cast-iron or nonstick skillet instead.

> 3 tablespoons balsamic vinegar
>
> 1 tablespoon plus 1 teaspoon extra-virgin olive oil
>
> 2 garlic cloves, minced
>
> ½ teaspoon dried thyme
>
> ¾ pound sirloin steak, ¾ to 1 inch thick
>
> Salt and freshly ground black pepper

Place vinegar, 1 tablespoon of the oil, garlic, and thyme in a large resealable plastic bag. Add steak and seal bag, pressing out the air. Shake sealed bag so that steak becomes coated with marinade. Refrigerate for 4 hours or overnight.

Heat a grill pan over medium-high heat. Brush steak lightly with remaining 1 teaspoon oil. Place steak on grill pan and cook 4 to 5 minutes per side for medium-rare, brushing with marinade as it cooks. Transfer steak to a cutting board; let rest for 5 minutes. Discard remaining marinade. Cut steak into thick slices and serve warm.

Makes 2 (6-ounce) servings

NUTRITION AT A GLANCE

Per serving: 310 calories, 14 g fat, 3.5 g saturated fat, 38 g protein, 7 g carbohydrate, 0 g fiber, 100 mg sodium

MAKE-AHEAD: Steak can be marinated up to 1 day in advance. Bring to room temperature before grilling.

Ruby Swiss Chard Sauté

PREP TIME: 15 minutes   **COOK TIME:** 10 minutes

Ruby chard's deep color invokes the sweetheart sentiment of the day. And its nutritional benefits—including ample beta-carotene, potassium, and vitamins E and K—are sure to seal the deal. If you can't find ruby red chard, try green chard or spinach instead.

- 1 tablespoon extra-virgin olive oil
- 1 garlic clove, thinly sliced
- 1 pound ruby Swiss chard, with tender stems, cut into ¼-inch-wide ribbons (4 to 5 cups)
- 2 tablespoons water

  Salt and freshly ground black pepper

Heat oil in a large nonstick skillet over medium-high heat. Add garlic, reduce heat to low, and cook, stirring occasionally, until garlic is fragrant and lightly golden, about 3 minutes. Add chard, water, and a pinch of salt; cover, increase heat to medium, and cook, stirring occasionally, until greens are tender, about 5 minutes. Season lightly with salt and pepper and serve hot.

Makes 2 (1-cup) servings

NUTRITION AT A GLANCE

Per serving: 110 calories, 7 g fat, 1 g saturated fat, 4 g protein, 9 g carbohydrate, 4 g fiber, 318 mg sodium

MAKE-AHEAD: You can trim tough stems from chard, then wash, spin dry, and chop up to 12 hours in advance. Loosely wrap in a paper towel, place in a resealable plastic bag, and refrigerate until ready to use. When making dinner, prepare the chard first; it will keep warm, covered, while you cook the steak.

TIP **Maximizing chard:** Chard stems are edible and very tasty; remove any tough parts and chop the tender stems along with the leaves.

Baked Tomatoes with Feta and Herbs

PREP TIME: 15 minutes   **COOK TIME:** 20 minutes

These warm, juicy tomato towers can be built in no time and get fantastic flavor from the addition of garlic, extra-virgin olive oil, and lemon zest. Use a toaster oven to bake them, if you prefer.

- 1   ounce reduced-fat feta cheese, crumbled
- 1   garlic clove, minced
- ¼   teaspoon dried oregano
- 1   teaspoon extra-virgin olive oil
- 1   teaspoon grated lemon zest
- 1   large ripe tomato, ends trimmed and cut crosswise into 4 slices

    Freshly ground black pepper

Heat oven to 400°F. Line a baking sheet with parchment or foil.

Combine feta, garlic, oregano, oil, and zest in a small bowl.

Place 2 tomato slices on the baking sheet. Top each slice with one-fourth of the feta mixture. Place a second tomato slice on top of each and cover with remaining feta mixture. Sprinkle with a little pepper.

Bake until heated through and feta is lightly golden, 18 to 20 minutes. Serve hot.

Makes 2 servings

NUTRITION AT A GLANCE

Per serving: 70 calories, 4 g fat, 1.5 g saturated fat, 4 g protein, 5 g carbohydrate, 1 g fiber, 190 mg sodium

MAKE-AHEAD: Tomato stacks can be assembled 1 hour in advance and kept covered at room temperature. Bake just before serving.

Grapefruit and Avocado Salad

PREP TIME: 15 minutes   **COOK TIME:** 10 minutes

An unexpected pairing, juicy grapefruit and creamy avocado create a lovely and very refreshing salad that will make even the stonyhearted swoon. Look for fleur de sel, a flavorful French sea salt, in gourmet shops. Or, you can lightly grind larger sea salt crystals for the perfect accent.

2   teaspoons shelled, unsalted pistachio nuts

1   small red or pink grapefruit

1   avocado

2   teaspoons extra-virgin olive oil

½   teaspoon red wine vinegar

⅛   teaspoon lightly ground sea salt

Freshly ground black pepper

Heat oven to 275°F. Spread nuts on a baking sheet and toast until fragrant and lightly golden, about 8 minutes. Transfer to a plate to cool slightly, then chop finely.

While nuts are toasting, segment grapefruit: Using a sharp paring knife, cut the ends off the top and bottom of the fruit, then cut off the peel. Holding grapefruit over a bowl to catch the juice, carefully cut along the membrane on both sides of each grapefruit segment. Allow the freed segments to fall into the bowl. Squeeze the remaining membrane over the bowl to extract additional juice.

Just before serving, halve avocado and remove pit and peel. Cut each avocado half into thin slices and fan slices on 2 salad plates. Reserving grapefruit juice, arrange half of the grapefruit segments decoratively around the avocado.

Whisk together oil, vinegar, and 1 teaspoon of the grapefruit juice in a small bowl. Drizzle half of the dressing over each salad. Sprinkle each salad with pistachios and salt. Season with pepper to taste and serve.

Makes 2 servings

NUTRITION AT A GLANCE
Per serving: 230 calories, 19 g fat, 2.5 g saturated fat, 3 g protein, 16 g carbohydrate, 7 g fiber, 150 mg sodium

MAKE-AHEAD: Nuts can be toasted up to 3 days ahead and kept refrigerated or at room temperature in an airtight container. Grapefruit can be segmented up to 12 hours ahead and refrigerated in a covered container.

Strawberry Blancmange

PREP TIME: 10 minutes   **COOK TIME:** 5 minutes   **CHILL TIME:** 2 hours or overnight

Similar to a Bavarian cream or Italian panna cotta, blancmange is an almond-flavored milk pudding, often thickened with gelatin. The name comes from the French blanc *(meaning "white") and* manger *(to eat).*

¾ teaspoon unflavored gelatin

2 tablespoons cold water

⅓ cup unsweetened almond milk

⅛ teaspoon almond extract

⅛ teaspoon vanilla extract

¼ cup light or fat-free whipped topping

1 cup diced strawberries

2 small perfect strawberries for garnish (optional)

Lightly coat 2 (½-cup) ramekins or heart-shaped molds with cooking spray.

Sprinkle gelatin over water in a cup and let stand for 2 minutes.

Meanwhile, heat almond milk in a small saucepan over low heat, until it comes to a bare simmer. Add gelatin mixture and cook, stirring constantly, until dissolved, about 1 minute. Stir in almond and vanilla extracts. Transfer to a small bowl set over a bowl of ice water and stir until the mixture is thickened slightly. Add the whipped topping and diced strawberries; stir to combine. Divide mixture between ramekins and chill for 2 hours or overnight.

When ready to serve, run a knife around the edge of the blancmange and, using your finger to help coax it from the ramekin, gently turn each out onto a plate. Top each blancmange with a whole strawberry, if desired, and serve.

Makes 2 servings

NUTRITION AT A GLANCE
Per serving: 60 calories, 1 g fat, 0 g saturated fat, 1 g protein, 10 g carbohydrate, 2 g fiber, 35 mg sodium

MAKE-AHEAD: Blancmange can be made up to 1 day in advance. Leave in molds, cover with plastic wrap, and refrigerate until ready to serve.

PASSOVER SEDER

FOR 8 GUESTS

Passover is celebrated over eight days, with a celebratory Seder held on the first two nights. This Jewish holiday commemorates the exodus of the Israelites from Egypt. Because they fled so quickly, they were only able to take unleavened bread with them. That is why leavened bread is not eaten during Passover and why matzoh is used in many of the traditional dishes.

To begin, we've included a recipe for haroset, made with tart apples, crunchy nuts, and sweet Passover wine. You'll use the healthy, whole-wheat version of both matzoh and matzoh meal to make tasty gefilte fish, light and flavorful matzoh balls, and a delectable chocolate-orange torte with a dreamy ganache glaze. A wonderful roast salmon and beautiful vegetable tian are both cooked using extra-virgin olive oil, making a nutritious and very tasty meal that guests young and old will love. When you make your shopping list, don't forget to include a shank bone to roast, an egg to hard-boil, parsley, and extra horseradish for the Seder plate.

◀ *No need to deviate from your South Beach Diet with this healthy holiday Seder, which pays attention to both taste and tradition.*

MENU

Haroset

Gefilte Fish with Horseradish

Matzoh Ball Soup

Roasted Salmon with Fennel and Lemon

Squash and Tomato Tian

Flourless Chocolate-Orange Torte

Holiday Game Plan

Up to 1 month before: Make and freeze stock for soup.

Up to 1 day before: Make gefilte fish; bake torte; thaw stock.

Day of: Make haroset; prepare salmon and tian; make glaze and glaze torte; make matzoh balls and heat stock.

Haroset

PREP TIME: 10 minutes

A mixture of diced apples, nuts, cinnamon, and sweet Passover wine, haroset is served at the Passover Seder to symbolize the mortar that the slaves used to build the pyramids of ancient Egypt. Almonds or pecans can be substituted for the walnuts, if you want to try something different. Sweet Passover wine in this recipe is in keeping with the holiday tradition and is appropriate for this special occasion.

   3 medium Granny Smith apples, chopped

  ⅔ cup walnuts

  ½ teaspoon ground cinnamon

  1 teaspoon grated lemon zest

  3 tablespoons sweet red Passover wine

Pulse apples, walnuts, cinnamon, zest, and wine in a food processor until well combined. Transfer to a shallow bowl and serve.

Makes 8 (generous ¼-cup) servings

NUTRITION AT A GLANCE

Per serving: 80 calories, 5 g fat, 0.5 g saturated fat, 2 g protein, 6 g carbohydrate, 2 g fiber, 15 mg sodium

MAKE-AHEAD: Haroset can be made up to 8 hours in advance and refrigerated in a covered container; bring to room temperature before serving.

Gefilte Fish with Horseradish

PREP TIME: 20 minutes   **COOK TIME:** 25 minutes   **CHILL TIME:** 3 hours or overnight

Carp, pike, and whitefish (a mild North American freshwater fish) are the classic combination in most gefilte fish recipes. Carp is usually available around Passover but is a little harder to find at other times of the year. You can easily prepare gefilte fish anytime using just pike and whitefish, or you can use cod or snapper as a substitute for carp.

5 cups vegetable broth	1 small carrot, halved crosswise
5 cups water	1 sheet whole-wheat matzoh
½ pound pike fillets, cut into chunks	1 large egg
½ pound whitefish fillets, cut into chunks	1 teaspoon granular sugar substitute
½ pound carp fillets, cut into chunks	1 teaspoon salt
	⅛ teaspoon ground white pepper
1 small onion, quartered	¼ cup prepared horseradish

Bring broth and water to a simmer in a large saucepan.

Meanwhile, process fish fillets in a food processor until finely chopped and smooth. Transfer to a large bowl; set aside.

Place onion, carrot, and matzoh in the food processor, and process until finely chopped; add to reserved fish. Add egg, sugar substitute, salt, and pepper; stir to combine. Using ⅓ cup of fish mixture for each patty, form 12 (3-inch) patties.

Carefully lower fish patties into the simmering broth. Cover and simmer gently until cooked through, about 20 minutes. Using a slotted spoon, remove patties and place in a single layer in a large baking dish. Pour enough of the cooking liquid over the fish to just cover. Refrigerate, covered, until chilled, about 3 hours or overnight. Remove patties from broth and serve chilled with prepared horseradish on the side.

Makes 12 patties

NUTRITION AT A GLANCE

Per patty (with 1 teaspoon horseradish): 92 calories, 3 g fat, 0.5 g saturated fat, 12 g protein, 6 g carbohydrate, 0 g fiber, 385 mg sodium

MAKE-AHEAD: Gefilte fish can be made up to 1 day in advance and refrigerated in the broth in a covered baking dish. Remove from broth before serving chilled.

Matzoh Ball Soup

PREP TIME: 25 minutes   **COOK TIME:** 3 hours

This rich soup is a Seder essential. Making your own chicken stock is the secret here, although you could use lower-sodium chicken broth if you're short on time. To make whole-wheat matzoh meal, process whole matzohs in a food processor until finely ground. You will need 3½ to 4 matzoh sheets to make 1 cup of matzoh meal.

Chicken stock

- 3 pounds split chicken breasts, skin removed
- 1 pound carrots, halved
- 3 celery stalks, cut into 2-inch pieces
- 1 large onion, unpeeled, cut into quarters
- 5 garlic cloves, unpeeled
- 1 (2-inch) piece fresh ginger
- 10 sprigs fresh thyme
- 1 teaspoon salt
- 10 cups water

Matzoh balls

- 1 cup whole-wheat matzoh meal
- 1 tablespoon canola oil
- ½ cup seltzer water
- 4 large eggs
- ½ teaspoon salt
- ¼ teaspoon freshly ground black pepper

Garnish

- 2 carrot halves, reserved from chicken broth, finely chopped
- 2 tablespoons chopped fresh dill

For the chicken stock: Place chicken, carrots, celery, onion, garlic, ginger, thyme, salt, and water in a large stockpot; bring to a boil over high heat. Reduce heat to a simmer and cook, skimming foam as needed, until stock is rich and flavorful, 2 to 2½ hours. Strain stock; reserve 2 carrot halves for garnish and the chicken meat for another use. Discard rest of solids. Return stock to stockpot. Skim off any visible fat.

For the matzoh balls: While chicken stock is simmering, combine matzoh meal, oil, and seltzer in a medium bowl. In a small bowl, whisk eggs, salt, and pepper until foamy. Stir egg mixture into matzoh mixture until well combined; cover with plastic wrap and refrigerate for 2 hours.

To cook matzoh balls: Bring 2 quarts of water to a boil in a large saucepan. Meanwhile, with wet hands to prevent sticking, form 16 walnut-size balls of chilled dough. Reduce water to a simmer, then gently lower matzoh balls into the simmering water using a slotted spoon. Cook until all the matzoh balls have floated to the top and are cooked through, about 25 minutes.

Meanwhile, bring chicken stock to a simmer. Divide stock and matzoh balls among 8 serving bowls, add a little chopped carrot and dill to each bowl, and serve.

Makes 8 servings

NUTRITION AT A GLANCE

Per serving (with 1 matzoh ball): 80 calories, 3 g fat, 1 g saturated fat, 4.5 g protein, 10 g carbohydrate, 1.5 g fiber, 400 mg sodium

Per serving (with 2 matzoh balls): 130 calories, 5 g fat, 1.5 g saturated fat, 7 g protein, 15 g carbohydrate, 2 g fiber, 490 mg sodium

MAKE-AHEAD: Stock can be made up to 2 days ahead and refrigerated in a covered container until ready to use. Or it can be frozen for up to 1 month. Skim off any fat that rises to the top before using.

Roasted Salmon with Fennel and Lemon

PREP TIME: 15 minutes   **COOK TIME:** 20 minutes

The ingredients in this tasty dish celebrate the spring season. Use a mandoline or very sharp chef's knife to slice the fennel as thin as possible; if sliced too thick, it will not cook through. Dill sprigs and extra lemon slices make an easy and lovely garnish.

2	(1½-pound) salmon tail-end fillets, about 1 inch thick
4	teaspoons extra-virgin olive oil
½	teaspoon salt
½	teaspoon freshly ground black pepper
1	small fennel bulb, very thinly sliced
1	lemon, thinly sliced
2	tablespoons chopped fresh dill
	Dill sprigs and lemon slices for garnish (optional)

Heat oven to 475°F.

Rinse salmon and pat dry. Using your fingers or tweezers, remove any small bones from the fillets. Rub oil all over the fillets (skin included). Sprinkle each fillet with salt and pepper.

Place one fillet, skin side down, on a wire rack over a baking pan, then layer fennel, lemon, and dill across the surface of the fillet. Place the remaining fillet, skin side up, on top of the first fillet. Using kitchen twine, tie the halves of the fish together so they stay in place while cooking.

Roast salmon (on the rack over the baking pan) until the skin appears lightly browned and fish is cooked through, about 20 minutes. Remove string, transfer to a serving platter, and serve hot.

Makes 8 (6-ounce) servings

NUTRITION AT A GLANCE
Per serving: 330 calories, 20 g fat, 4 g saturated fat, 34 g protein, 2 g carbohydrate, 0 g fiber, 260 mg sodium

MAKE-AHEAD: Salmon can be assembled and tied up to 8 hours in advance; wrap in plastic wrap and refrigerate. Remove from refrigerator 30 minutes before baking.

Squash and Tomato Tian

PREP TIME: 12 minutes   **COOK TIME:** 40 minutes

Tian is a French Provençal dish of vegetables, baked gratin-style. Look for zucchini and yellow summer squash of similar lengths so that you get a fairly even number of slices. Try rosemary, oregano, or basil (or a combination of these) as an option to thyme, if you like.

  3 teaspoons extra-virgin olive oil

  ½ teaspoon dried thyme

  ½ teaspoon salt

  ¼ teaspoon freshly ground black pepper

  3 medium zucchini, thinly sliced

  3 medium yellow summer squash, thinly sliced

  6 plum tomatoes, thinly sliced

Heat oven to 400°F.

Brush a 9- by 13-inch baking dish with 1 teaspoon of the oil. Combine thyme, salt, and pepper in a small bowl. Combine zucchini and summer squash in a medium bowl.

Place half of the squash mixture in the baking dish and sprinkle with one-third of the thyme mixture. Top with tomatoes and sprinkle with half of the remaining thyme mixture. Top with remaining squash and sprinkle with remaining thyme mixture. Drizzle top layer with remaining 2 teaspoons oil.

Bake until vegetables are tender, 30 to 40 minutes. Serve warm.

Makes 8 (1-cup) servings

NUTRITION AT A GLANCE
Per serving: 45 calories, 2 g fat, 0 g saturated fat, 2 g protein, 7 g carbohydrate, 2 g fiber, 160 mg sodium

MAKE-AHEAD: The tian can be assembled in the baking dish up to 12 hours in advance. Refrigerate, covered, until ready to bake.

Flourless Chocolate-Orange Torte

PREP TIME: 20 minutes   **COOK TIME:** 50 minutes   **COOLING TIME:** 35 minutes

Chocolate, matzoh cake meal, and nuts are popular ingredients in Passover desserts. This memorable torte contains all three, plus the addition of orange for extra sweetness.

Torte

½ cup trans-fat-free margarine

¼ cup granular sugar substitute

4 eggs, separated

¾ cup ground almonds

½ cup matzoh cake meal

4 ounces bittersweet chocolate, finely chopped

½ teaspoon vanilla extract

1 teaspoon grated orange zest

¼ cup fresh orange juice

Sliced almonds (optional)

Glaze

¼ cup fat-free half-and-half

¼ cup bittersweet chocolate chips

For the torte: Heat oven to 325°F. Line an 8-inch cake pan with wax paper.

Using a wooden spoon, cream margarine and sugar substitute together in a large bowl until light and fluffy. Whisk in egg yolks. Stir in almonds, matzoh meal, chocolate, vanilla, zest, and orange juice (batter will be thick).

In another large bowl, with an electric mixer at high speed, beat egg whites until they form stiff peaks. Gently fold whites into chocolate batter. Turn batter into pan and bake until a tester inserted in the center comes out clean, 40 to 45 minutes. Cool torte in the pan on a wire rack for 5 minutes, then turn out onto the rack and cool for another 30 minutes.

For the glaze: When torte has cooled, combine half-and-half and chocolate chips in a small saucepan. Cook over low heat, stirring constantly, until chocolate is melted and mixture is slightly thickened, 2 to 3 minutes. Remove from heat and let stand for 2 minutes. Spread glaze over top of cake. Garnish with sliced almonds, if using.

Makes 12 servings

NUTRITION AT A GLANCE

Per serving: 200 calories, 16 g fat, 5 g saturated fat, 5 g protein, 13 g carbohydrate, 2 g fiber, 90 mg sodium

MAKE-AHEAD: Torte without glaze can be made up to 1 day ahead; refrigerate and bring to room temperature before serving. Glaze with ganache up to 8 hours before serving.

EASTER GATHERING

FOR 8 GUESTS

Cheerful decorations and sumptuous foods abound at Easter. The season brings plenty of healthy fresh spring vegetables to the table, each offering a different vibrant color and flavor. Here you'll use them to make gorgeous zucchini rounds, each simply roasted with a tiny cherry tomato for the perfect start to the meal. There's also a sweet puréed carrot soup; a lemony quinoa salad with crisp bits of celery and cucumber; tender snap peas tossed with olive oil and fresh strips of mint; and a juicy roast leg of lamb. A refreshing mocktail, made with mint and ginger, can be served before or with the meal.

Fresh spring flowers, such as lilies, lilacs, daffodils, and tulips, speak to the season and can be placed on the dining table and around the house. Small pots of crocuses can be used for both table decor and as parting gifts for guests. Dyed eggs, of course, are apropos and extra fun to make when children get involved.

◀ *Carrot soup with a swirl of light sour cream is the perfect starter for this elegant Easter meal. Mint-ginger spritzers provide a flavorful counterpoint.*

MENU

Roasted Zucchini Bites

Carrot Soup

Snap Peas with Mint

Spring Quinoa Salad

*Herb and Garlic Roasted
Leg of Lamb*

Raspberry "Shortcakes"

Mint-Ginger Spritzers

Holiday Game Plan

Up to 1 week before: Make syrup for spritzers.

Up to 1 day before: Make soup and quinoa salad.

Day of: Make shortcakes; make zucchini bites; roast lamb; make snap peas; make spritzers.

Roasted Zucchini Bites

PREP TIME: 20 minutes   **COOK TIME:** 25 minutes

These pretty starters are made even more festive if you use a mix of red, orange, and yellow cherry tomatoes. You can also try grape or pear tomatoes, which differ in shape from cherry. Use whichever end of a melon baller is appropriate to the size of your zucchini pieces to get a perfect pocket for the tomatoes.

3 medium (8-inch) zucchini	¼ teaspoon dried thyme
2 tablespoons extra-virgin olive oil	Salt and freshly ground black pepper
¾ teaspoon dried basil	24 cherry tomatoes

Position rack in middle of oven and heat oven to 425°F.

Slice just the tips off the rounded ends of the zucchini. Cut each zucchini crosswise into 8 (1-inch-thick) rounds. Using a melon baller, scoop a pocket into each piece of zucchini (do not scoop all the way through).

Whisk together oil, basil, and thyme in a large bowl. Add zucchini pieces and toss to coat. Season lightly with salt and generously with pepper.

Transfer zucchini pieces, with the pocket facing up, to a baking sheet; reserve any oil mixture left in the bowl. Place tomatoes in the same bowl and, using your hands, toss gently to coat with the remaining oil mixture.

Place 1 tomato in each zucchini pocket. Using a rubber spatula, scrape all of the remaining oil and seasonings over the zucchini bites.

Bake until the bottoms and tops are golden, about 25 minutes. Let cool about 10 minutes and serve warm.

Makes 8 (3-piece) servings

NUTRITION AT A GLANCE
Per serving: 50 calories, 3.5 g fat, 0.5 g saturated fat, 1 g protein, 5 g carbohydrate, 1 g fiber, 10 mg sodium

MAKE-AHEAD: Zucchini bites can be made up to 6 hours in advance; cover and refrigerate until ready to use. Warm through in a 325°F oven for 5 to 10 minutes just before serving.

Carrot Soup

PREP TIME: 15 minutes   **COOK TIME:** 40 minutes

This creamy, rich soup has a brilliant orange hue that brings gorgeous color to the Easter table. Add a bit of water or extra broth if you prefer a thinner soup.

3 tablespoons extra-virgin olive oil

1 medium sweet onion or yellow onion, roughly chopped

3 garlic cloves, smashed and peeled

2½ pounds carrots, cut into ½-inch pieces

4 cups lower-sodium chicken broth

2 cups water

Ground white pepper

8 teaspoons reduced-fat sour cream

Mint sprigs for garnish

Heat oil in a large saucepan over medium-high heat. Add onion and garlic; stir to coat. Reduce heat to medium-low and cook, stirring occasionally, until they soften, about 10 minutes. Add carrots, stir to coat, and cook for 10 minutes. Add broth and water, and bring to a boil. Reduce heat to medium-low and simmer until carrots are tender, 10 to 12 minutes.

Purée soup in a blender or food processor. Season with pepper to taste. Serve hot with a teaspoon of sour cream and sprig of mint in each bowl.

Makes 8 (1-cup) servings

NUTRITION AT A GLANCE

Per serving: 130 calories, 6 g fat, 1 g saturated fat, 3 g protein, 16 g carbohydrate, 4 g fiber, 380 mg sodium

MAKE-AHEAD: Soup can be made up to 1 day ahead and refrigerated in a covered container.

Snap Peas with Mint

PREP TIME: 20 minutes   **COOK TIME:** 15 minutes

A lovely and classic spring combination gets a slight twist with the use of snap peas in place of the usual green peas. You can also use snow peas, if you wish.

1½ pounds snap peas, trimmed

2 tablespoons extra-virgin olive oil

3 tablespoons red onion

¼ cup thinly sliced fresh mint leaves

Salt and freshly ground black pepper

Heat oil in a large nonstick skillet over medium heat. Add red onion, reduce heat to medium-low, and cook until softened, about 3 minutes. Stir in snap peas. Increase heat to medium-high and stir-fry about 3 minutes. Stir in mint; season with salt and pepper to taste, and serve hot.

Makes 8 (½-cup) servings

NUTRITION AT A GLANCE
Per serving: 70 calories, 3.5 g fat, 0.5 g saturated fat, 2 g protein, 7 g carbohydrate, 2 g fiber, 10 mg sodium

PHASE 2

Spring Quinoa Salad

PREP TIME: 15 minutes   **COOK TIME:** 20 minutes

Quinoa—pronounced "keen-wa"—is easy to cook and is a good source of the cell-protecting amino acid lysine, as well as potassium and magnesium.

⅓ cup plus 2 tablespoons fresh lemon juice

¼ cup plus 2 tablespoons minced red onion

¾ teaspoon salt

4 cups water

2 cups quinoa, rinsed

1 large cucumber, peeled, seeded, and finely chopped

2 celery stalks, finely chopped

⅓ cup chopped fresh mint

Black pepper

Stir together lemon juice, onion, and salt in a small bowl; set aside.

Bring water to a boil in a medium saucepan. Add quinoa and reduce heat to low; cover and gently simmer until tender, about 15 minutes. Drain any excess water. Spread quinoa on a baking sheet to cool.

Transfer cooled quinoa to a serving bowl. Add cucumber, celery, mint, lemon juice mixture, and pepper to taste; toss to combine. Serve at room temperature.

Makes 8 (¾-cup) servings

NUTRITION AT A GLANCE
Per serving: 170 calories, 2.5 g fat, 0 g saturated fat, 6 g protein, 33 g carbohydrate, 3 g fiber, 240 mg sodium

MAKE-AHEAD: Salad can be made up to 1 day ahead and refrigerated in a covered container.

Herb and Garlic Roasted Leg of Lamb

PREP TIME: 15 minutes   **COOK TIME:** 1 hour 20 minutes   **RESTING TIME:** 15 minutes

Nothing says Easter like an herb- and garlic-infused leg of lamb, served here with a savory Dijon mustard coating. Ask your butcher to bone and tie the lamb for you.

1 (3-pound) boneless sirloin leg of lamb, tied

   Salt and freshly ground black pepper

1 tablespoon plus 1½ teaspoons chopped fresh rosemary

1 tablespoon plus 1½ teaspoons chopped fresh thyme

1 tablespoon chopped fresh parsley

2 garlic cloves, minced

¼ cup Dijon mustard

Heat oven to 350°F.

Sprinkle lamb lightly on all sides with salt and pepper. Combine rosemary, thyme, parsley, and garlic in a small bowl. Cut ½-inch-deep slits in the thickest parts of the leg and fill the cuts with the herbs, pressing the mixture in with your finger.

Lightly coat a large skillet with cooking spray and heat over medium-high heat. Brown lamb on all sides, about 5 minutes per side. Remove lamb from skillet and transfer to a roasting pan. Coat with mustard on all sides. Roast until lamb reaches 135°F (for medium-rare) on a meat thermometer, about 1 hour.

Remove from oven, cover loosely with foil, and allow to rest for 15 minutes before slicing. Serve warm.

Makes 8 (6-ounce) servings

NUTRITION AT A GLANCE
Per serving: 230 calories, 9 g fat, 3.5 g saturated fat, 35 g protein, 0 g carbohydrate, 0 g fiber, 240 mg sodium

TIP **Carving a boneless leg of lamb:** After you've let the roasted lamb rest for 15 minutes, position it horizontally on your cutting board. Snip the strings with a pair of kitchen shears, then remove and discard them. Using a sharp carving knife and a gentle sawing motion, slice the lamb in thick or thin slices (as you like) across the grain. Serve the sliced lamb with its delicious juices.

Raspberry "Shortcakes"

PREP TIME: 30 minutes   **COOK TIME:** 25 minutes

This stunning dessert recalls the traditional American strawberry shortcake—with its sweet berries and fluffy light cream. The cake is best made on the day of the party.

Cake

- 1½ cups whole-grain pastry flour
- ½ teaspoon baking soda
- ½ teaspoon baking powder
- ¼ teaspoon salt
- 3 large eggs, separated
- ½ cup 1% or fat-free buttermilk
- ½ cup extra-virgin olive oil
- ½ cup granular sugar substitute
- 1 tablespoon grated lemon zest
- 2 teaspoons lemon extract

Topping

- 1 cup low-fat plain yogurt
- 1 cup fat-free or light whipped topping
- 2 cups fresh raspberries

For the cake: Heat oven to 350°F. Lightly coat a 7- by 11-inch baking pan with cooking spray.

Whisk together flour, baking soda, baking powder, and salt in a large bowl; form a well in the center.

In a medium large bowl, with an electric mixer at high speed, beat egg whites until stiff peaks form, about 3 minutes; set aside.

In another medium bowl, with electric mixer at medium speed, beat egg yolks, buttermilk, oil, sugar substitute, zest, and lemon extract until smooth, about 1 minute. Pour yolk mixture into center of dry ingredients; stir gently until just combined. Gently fold in half of the egg whites to lighten the batter, then fold in the remaining whites until just combined.

Pour batter into pan and bake until edges are lightly brown and a tester inserted in the center comes out clean, 20 to 22 minutes. Let cake cool in pan; remove from pan and transfer to wire rack to cool completely. When ready to serve, cut cooled cake into 8 (2½- by 3½-inch) pieces.

For the topping: Just before serving, place yogurt in a small bowl and fold in whipped topping. Spoon ¼ cup topping and ¼ cup raspberries onto each piece of cake and serve.

Makes 8 servings

NUTRITION AT A GLANCE
Per serving: 290 calories, 17 g fat, 3 g saturated fat, 7 g protein, 27 g carbohydrate, 4 g fiber, 170 mg sodium

Mint-Ginger Spritzers

PREP TIME: 5 minutes   **COOK TIME:** 10 minutes   **STEEPING TIME:** 4 hours

A natural pair, ginger and mint are the base for this refreshing drink, which can be served as a predinner mocktail or as the perfect complement to the whole Easter meal. Serve the spritzers in pretty, tall glasses or in large martini glasses (without ice), if you prefer. This recipe makes extra syrup, which can be used if your guests want seconds or stored it in a sealed container in the refrigerator for up to a week.

> 3 tablespoons roughly chopped fresh ginger
>
> ½ cup water
>
> 3 tablespoons granular sugar substitute
>
> 1 cup fresh mint leaves
>
> 1 (2-liter) bottle seltzer water, chilled
>
>   Ice cubes
>
> 8 small fresh mint sprigs

Place ginger in a small saucepan with water and sugar substitute. Bring to a simmer, remove from heat, and let steep in saucepan at room temperature for at least 4 hours.

After ginger syrup has steeped, add mint leaves and bring to a boil. Remove from heat and cool to room temperature. Strain.

To serve, pour ½ cup of seltzer into a glass, add 1 tablespoon mint–ginger syrup, and stir. Add ice and stir again. Top drink with a mint sprig. Repeat for remaining drinks.

Makes 8 (½-cup) drinks

NUTRITION AT A GLANCE

Per drink: 0 calories, 0 g fat, 0 g saturated fat, 0 g protein, 0 g carbohydrate, 0 g fiber, 0 mg sodium

MAKE-AHEAD: Mint-ginger syrup can be made up to 1 week in advance and stored in a covered container in the refrigerator until ready to use.

CINCO DE MAYO CELEBRATION

FOR 8 GUESTS

Music, dancing, colorful decorations, and festive food are all part of Cinco de Mayo (Fifth of May), the Mexican holiday that commemorates the country's victory over a French army twice its size at the famous Battle of Puebla on that day in 1862. Today it is a spirited occasion that is fun to celebrate with a fabulous Mexican meal and a big group of friends.

Creamy avocado, sweet and spicy peppers, crunchy jícama, mango, and cilantro are just some of the popular Mexican ingredients you'll use to create a refreshing homemade salsa, two sumptuous salads, tasty chicken tacos, and more. Your guests will want to use the salsa and dip as toppings for the tacos, too.

For table decor, go for bright color; a Mexican blanket or a pretty woven runner makes a great tablecloth. Look for maracas, crepe-paper flowers, piñatas, and sombreros at party supply shops. Be sure to play some south-of-the-border music and push back the furniture to make room for a lively Mexican hat dance!

◄ *Mexican food can easily be part of the South Beach Diet when each dish is prepared with the freshest, healthiest ingredients.*

MENU

Endive Spears with
Fresh Pepper Salsa

Grilled Shrimp
with Chipotle Dip

Guacamole Salad

Jícama and Orange Salad

Soft Chicken Tacos

Spicy Frijoles

Mexican-Style Rice

Mango-Lime Fools

Holiday Game Plan

Up to 1 month ahead: Make and freeze rice.

Up to 1 day before: Thaw rice; make dip for shrimp; make dressing for guacamole salad; prepare vegetables for jícama salad; cook chicken and peppers for tacos; make beans; cube mangos for fools.

Day of: Make salsa; marinate shrimp; finish tacos and rice; assemble salads and endive spears with salsa; make fools; grill shrimp.

Endive Spears with Fresh Pepper Salsa

PREP TIME: 20 minutes

Bold and cheerful, these spears add a burst of color and flavor to your party table. Of course, there are countless salsas (both fresh and in jars) available at the super-market, but nothing tastes as good as homemade. Our version includes a bright yellow bell pepper for texture and flavor. Put extra salsa out in bowls for your guests to spoon over the tacos.

- 3 medium tomatoes, chopped, with juices reserved
- 1 medium yellow bell pepper, finely chopped
- 2 large scallions, chopped
- 3 tablespoons finely chopped fresh cilantro
- 2 tablespoons fresh lime juice
- 1 small serrano pepper or jalapeño, seeded and minced
- 1 garlic clove, minced
- ¼ teaspoon salt
- 3 medium heads Belgian endive, separated into 24 largest leaves

Stir together tomatoes, bell pepper, scallions, cilantro, lime juice, serrano chile, garlic, and salt in a medium bowl. Cover and refrigerate until ready to serve.

Arrange the endive leaves on a platter in a circular pattern. Place 1 heaping teaspoon salsa in the base of each leaf. Reserve the remaining salsa to spoon over the chicken tacos (page 160), if desired.

Makes 8 (3-piece) servings

NUTRITION AT A GLANCE
Per serving: 5 calories, 0 g fat, 0 g saturated fat, 0 g protein, 1 g carbohydrate, 0 g fiber, 20 mg sodium

MAKE-AHEAD: Salsa can be made up to 8 hours ahead. Refrigerate, covered, until ready to use.

Grilled Shrimp with Chipotle Dip

PREP TIME: 20 minutes   **MARINATING TIME:** At least 1 hour   **COOK TIME:** 10 minutes

Smoky chipotle peppers create a delicious dip that's even more flavorful after it sits in the fridge for a few hours or overnight. The chilies vary in heat and mellow as the dip sits, so taste before serving and adjust the amount of spice, if necessary. Canned chipotles are available in supermarkets or ethnic grocers; they come in adobo, a thick, piquant sauce made from ground chilies, vinegar, and herbs.

Shrimp

- 3 tablespoons fresh lime juice
- 2 tablespoons extra-virgin olive oil
- ¼ cup chopped fresh cilantro
- 3 scallions, chopped
- 2 garlic cloves, minced
  Salt
- 24 medium shrimp, peeled and deveined

Chipotle Dip

- 1½ cups nonfat or low-fat plain yogurt
- ⅓ cup reduced-fat sour cream
- 1–2 canned chipotle chilies in adobo
- 1 tablespoon fresh lime juice
  Salt

For the shrimp. Combine lime juice, oil, cilantro, scallions, garlic, and a pinch of salt in a resealable plastic bag. Add shrimp and toss to coat. Marinate in the refrigerator at least 1 hour or up to 8 hours, turning occasionally.

For the chipotle dip: While shrimp are marinating, purée yogurt, sour cream, chilies, and lime juice in a food processor or blender; adjust heat by adding some of the adobo sauce from the can, if desired. Add salt to taste. Cover and refrigerate until ready to serve.

Heat a grill or grill pan to medium-high. Drain marinade from shrimp and discard. Working in batches, if necessary, grill shrimp until just opaque, about 3 minutes per side. Serve warm or at room temperature with dip.

Makes 8 (3-piece) servings and 2 cups dip

NUTRITION AT A GLANCE
Per serving (with 4 tablespoons dip): 90 calories, 5 g fat, 1.5 g saturated fat, 6 g protein, 6 g carbohydrate, 0 g fiber, 65 mg sodium

MAKE-AHEAD: Dip is even better when made 1 day in advance. Refrigerate in a covered container, then whisk and adjust flavors before serving, if necessary. Shrimp can be marinated up to 8 hours ahead and cooked just before guests arrive.

Guacamole Salad

PREP TIME: 25 minutes

Peppery watercress, creamy avocado, juicy tomatoes, and tangy lime juice make a delightfully festive salad that will disappear fast!

2½ tablespoons fresh lime juice

1 tablespoon minced red onion

Salt

¼ cup chopped fresh cilantro

3 tablespoons extra-virgin olive oil

2 scallions, chopped

1 garlic clove, minced

2 (4-ounce) bunches watercress, thick stems removed

Freshly ground black pepper

3 large ripe tomatoes, diced, with juices reserved

2 medium avocados, pitted, peeled, and diced

Whisk together lime juice, onion, and ⅛ teaspoon salt in a small bowl; let sit at room temperature for 10 minutes. Add cilantro, oil, scallions, and garlic; whisk to combine.

Place watercress in a large serving bowl. Add dressing and toss gently; season to taste with salt and pepper. Add tomatoes and their juices and avocados; gently toss again and serve.

Makes 8 (1-cup) servings

NUTRITION AT A GLANCE

Per serving: 60 calories, 5 g fat, 1 g saturated fat, 1 g protein, 4 g carbohydrate, 1 g fiber, 50 mg sodium

MAKE-AHEAD: Dressing can be made up to 1 day in advance and refrigerated in a covered container. Bring to room temperature and whisk before using.

TIP **Pitting avocados:** For easy pitting, cut the avocado lengthwise to the pit, around the entire circumference. Twist in opposite directions to separate the two halves. Carefully whack the pit with a sharp blade, then twist and remove.

Jícama and Orange Salad

PREP TIME: 25 minutes

Jícama is a white-fleshed root vegetable with a slightly sweet and nutty taste. Its crisp, crunchy texture makes it perfect for salads, but it is also good cooked. Combined with juicy segmented oranges (see recipe directions on page 131 for how to section a fruit), chopped fresh cilantro, and jalapeño, it's a real treat.

1½	pounds jícama, peeled and cut into ½-inch dice
3	navel oranges, sectioned
2	medium cucumbers, peeled, seeded, and cut into ½-inch pieces
½	cup chopped fresh cilantro
¼	cup finely chopped red onion
1	medium jalapeño, seeded and minced
2	tablespoons extra-virgin olive oil
1	tablespoon plus 1 teaspoon red wine vinegar
	Salt

Toss together jícama, orange sections, cucumbers, cilantro, onion, jalapeño, oil, and vinegar in a serving bowl. Season with salt to taste and serve.

Makes 8 (1-cup) servings

NUTRITION AT A GLANCE
Per serving: 90 calories, 4 g fat, 0.5 g saturated fat, 1 g protein, 15 g carbohydrate, 2 g fiber, 5 mg sodium

MAKE-AHEAD: Oranges, cucumbers, and jícama can be prepared up to 1 day in advance and stored separately in resealable plastic bags with the air pressed out; toss with remaining ingredients just before serving.

Soft Chicken Tacos

PREP TIME: 10 minutes   **MARINATING TIME:** 30 minutes   **COOK TIME:** 20 minutes

Chicken flavored with fresh garlic, lime, and cilantro makes a traditional filling for these mini fold-ups.

- 4 (6-ounce) boneless, skinless chicken breasts
- 2 tablespoons plus 1 teaspoon extra-virgin olive oil
- 2 tablespoons fresh lime juice
- 2 medium garlic cloves, minced
- ¼ teaspoon salt
- ⅛ teaspoon freshly ground black pepper
- 3 medium red bell peppers, cut into thin strips
- 6 (8-inch) whole-wheat tortillas
- ¼ cup reduced-fat sour cream
- ¼ cup chopped fresh cilantro
- 1 lime, cut into 8 wedges

Arrange chicken snugly in a baking dish. Whisk together 2 tablespoons of the oil, lime juice, garlic, salt, and black pepper in a small bowl; pour marinade over chicken and turn to coat. Cover and refrigerate for 30 minutes.

Heat a grill or grill pan to medium-high. Remove chicken from marinade and grill until cooked through, about 5 minutes per side. Discard remaining marinade. Transfer chicken to a plate, cover loosely, and keep warm.

Brush bell peppers with remaining 1 teaspoon oil and grill until softened and lightly charred, about 5 minutes. Transfer to a plate, cover loosely, and keep warm. Grill tortillas, in batches, to make pliable, about 30 seconds per side. Cut each tortilla into quarters.

Cut chicken crosswise on the bias to make 24 thin slices; cut slices in half, if desired. Arrange tortilla pieces on a serving platter. Spoon ½ teaspoon sour cream onto each tortilla quarter. Divide chicken, peppers, and cilantro among tortillas. Serve warm with lime wedges.

Makes 8 (3-piece) servings

NUTRITION AT A GLANCE
Per serving: 210 calories, 7 g fat, 1.5 g saturated fat, 23 g protein, 19 g carbohydrate, 2 g fiber, 260 mg sodium

MAKE-AHEAD: Chicken and peppers can be grilled and refrigerated separately in covered containers up to 1 day ahead. Warm gently on stove top or in microwave before serving.

Spicy Frijoles

PREP TIME: 10 minutes   **COOK TIME:** 15 minutes

Beans, or frijoles in Spanish, are an important staple in the Mexican diet. Rich in flavor and texture, they make a terrific complement to the rest of this menu. But that's not all. These complex carbohydrates offer a wealth of nutritional benefits, including low-fat protein, fiber, B vitamins, and minerals. Remember to put out the hot sauce so that guests can adjust the heat to their liking.

3   tablespoons extra-virgin olive oil

1   medium onion, chopped

2   garlic cloves, minced

1   small serrano pepper or jalapeño, seeded and chopped

2   (15-ounce) cans pinto beans, rinsed and drained

1   (15-ounce) can black beans, rinsed and drained

1   tablespoon water

⅓   cup chopped fresh cilantro

1   tablespoon fresh lime juice

¼   teaspoon salt

    Hot pepper sauce

Heat oil in a medium saucepan over medium-high heat. Add onion, garlic, and serrano; reduce heat to low and cook, stirring occasionally, until onion is softened, 5 to 7 minutes.

Add beans and water; cover and cook until beans are heated through, about 5 minutes. Stir in cilantro, lime juice, and salt. Serve warm with hot sauce on the side.

Makes 8 (generous ½-cup) servings

NUTRITION AT A GLANCE

Per serving: 150 calories, 6 g fat, 1 g saturated fat, 6 g protein, 19 g carbohydrate, 6 g fiber, 350 mg sodium

MAKE-AHEAD: Beans become even more flavorful made 1 day in advance. Refrigerate beans in a covered container until ready to use, then gently reheat in a double boiler or microwave before serving.

Mexican-Style Rice

PREP TIME: 20 minutes   **COOK TIME:** 45 minutes

A meal without rice in Mexico is like a party without a piñata. Here cumin, cayenne, green pepper, fresh lime juice, and garlic flavor a nutritious pot of brown rice that will probably vanish before you can say "olé!" Use parboiled, quick-cooking whole-grain brown rice to save time, if you'd like—just make sure to purchase a brand that doesn't contain partially hydrogenated oils.

2 cups brown rice

2 tablespoons extra-virgin olive oil

2 medium green bell peppers, roughly chopped

1 large onion, roughly chopped

4 garlic cloves, minced

½ teaspoon ground cumin

¼ teaspoon cayenne pepper

2 tablespoons fresh lime juice

¼ teaspoon salt

1 medium tomato, roughly chopped

¼ cup chopped fresh cilantro (optional)

Cook rice according to package instructions.

While rice is cooking, heat oil in a large nonstick skillet over medium-high heat. Add bell peppers, onion, garlic, cumin, and cayenne; stir to combine. Reduce heat to medium low and cook, stirring occasionally, until vegetables are well softened, 14 to 16 minutes. Remove from heat.

When rice is cooked, fluff with a fork and transfer to a serving bowl. Stir in pepper mixture, lime juice, and salt. Top with chopped tomato and cilantro, if using, and serve.

Makes 12 (½-cup) servings

NUTRITION AT A GLANCE
Per serving: 150 calories, 3.5 g fat, 0.5 g saturated fat, 3 g protein, 27 g carbohydrate, 2 g fiber, 55 mg sodium

MAKE-AHEAD: Mexican rice can be prepared up to 1 day ahead and refrigerated in a covered container until ready to use. Heat gently in a double boiler or microwave before serving. You can make just the brown rice up to 2 days ahead and refrigerate. Or it can be frozen for up to 1 month. Defrost, if frozen, and heat through completely before mixing with remaining ingredients.

Mango-Lime Fools

PREP TIME: 20 minutes

A classic and very refreshing dessert, a fool is a fruit and cream mixture, traditionally made with gooseberries. We've given it a south-of-the-border flair with fresh cubes of juicy mango and lime. Present the desserts in small glass bowls or large martini glasses so the beautiful layers can be seen.

3 ripe mangos, peeled, seeded, and cut into ¼-inch cubes (2 cups)

2 tablespoons fresh lime juice

1 cup light or fat-free whipped topping

1 lime, cut into 8 thin slices

Toss together mangos and 1 tablespoon of the lime juice in a medium bowl. In a small bowl, whisk together whipped topping and remaining 1 tablespoon lime juice.

Place 2 tablespoons of mango mixture in each bowl or glass; top each with 2 tablespoons whipped topping, another 2 tablespoons mango mixture, and 1 lime slice. Serve immediately.

Makes 8 servings

NUTRITION AT A GLANCE

Per serving: 70 calories, 0 g fat, 0 g saturated fat, 0 g protein, 16 g carbohydrate, 1 g fiber, 5 mg sodium

MAKE-AHEAD: Mango can be cubed up to 1 day ahead and kept refrigerated in a covered container. You can also toss it with the lime juice up to 4 hours ahead and return to the refrigerator until ready to use.

TIP **Cubing a mango:** This process may seem intimidating but with a little practice you'll be a pro in no time. With a sharp paring knife, cut through the mango lengthwise, as close to the center seed as possible to create two halves. Cup a mango half in your palm, then score the flesh with the paring knife down to the skin in a crosshatch pattern. Be careful not to slit the outer skin. Bend the skin backward so the center pops up and the diamond-cut cubes are exposed. Cut the cubes off the skin and then remove any fruit still attached to the seed.

MOTHER'S DAY LUNCHEON

FOR 4 GUESTS

Cards and phone calls are nice, but why not do something extra special for Mom (or Grandmom!) on Mother's Day? She'll be thrilled when you invite her to have lunch with you and make clear she won't be doing a bit of the cooking.

This fantastic menu is easy to prepare and filled with nutritious dishes that will show Mom that you care not only for her but also for her health. The lemony broiled halibut provides lean protein. Tasty broccolini supplies plenty of calcium. And whole-wheat couscous is a good source of fiber. When you put all these ingredients together in this elegant meal, Mom is sure to be impressed.

After lunch, make time for a conversation-filled walk together. And remember, if you're preparing this meal in your mother's home, take care to clean up the pots, pans, and dishes afterward. That might be the best gift of all. Bringing flowers wouldn't hurt either.

◄ *Lemon ices with a hint of thyme and a touch of lemon zest make a lovely ending to a celebratory meal.*

MENU

Green Apple Spritzers

Zucchini Soup with Basil Cream

Fresh Crab Salad

Couscous with Toasted Pistachios

Broiled Halibut with Lemon and Dill

Broccolini with Warm Sun-Dried Tomato Vinaigrette

Lemon-Thyme Ices

Holiday Game Plan

Up to 1 month ahead: Cook and freeze couscous.

Up to 1 day before: Make soup and basil cream; prepare crab salad; cook broccolini; thaw couscous.

Day of: Make spritzers; assemble salad; finish couscous and broccolini; cook halibut; make ices.

Green Apple Spritzers

PREP TIME: 10 minutes

This fresh-tasting aperitif has a subtle, not-too-sweet fruit flavor. It's perfect for making a toast to Mom. Have the lemon juice ready before you slice the apple, since tossing the cut fruit with it will keep the apple from browning.

1	large Granny Smith apple
1	teaspoon fresh lemon juice
3	tablespoons ice water
1½	teaspoons granular sugar substitute
	Ice cubes
24	ounces seltzer water

Cut 8 very thin wedges from apple; core, peel, and roughly chop the rest. Toss apple wedges with ½ teaspoon of the lemon juice in a small bowl. In a separate small bowl, toss chopped apple with the remaining ½ teaspoon lemon juice.

Purée chopped apples, water, and sugar substitute in a blender. Divide puréed apple mixture among 4 glasses (about 2 tablespoons each); top each with a few ice cubes and fill each glass with seltzer. Stir, top each spritzer with 2 apple wedges, and serve.

Makes 4 (¾-cup) drinks

NUTRITION AT A GLANCE
Per drink: 20 calories, 0 g fat, 0 g saturated fat, 0 g protein, 6 g carbohydrate, 0 g fiber, 0 mg sodium

Zucchini Soup with Basil Cream

PREP TIME: 10 minutes   **COOK TIME:** 30 minutes

A simple zucchini soup becomes extra special with a swirl of fresh basil cream, which you can also try with other puréed vegetable soups.

Soup

- 2 tablespoons extra-virgin olive oil
- 1 small red onion, finely chopped
- 3 garlic cloves, minced
- ¼ teaspoon dried thyme
- ⅛ teaspoon ground cumin
- ⅛ teaspoon salt
- Red pepper flakes
- 2 medium zucchini, trimmed, and roughly chopped
- 2½ cups vegetable broth

Basil Cream

- 3 tablespoons reduced-fat sour cream
- 2 tablespoons chopped fresh basil
- 2 teaspoons fresh lemon juice
- Salt and freshly ground black pepper

For the soup: Heat oil in a medium saucepan over medium-high heat. Add onion, garlic, thyme, cumin, salt, and a pinch of pepper flakes. Reduce heat to medium-low and cook until onion has softened, about 8 minutes. Add zucchini, stir to coat, and cook for 1 minute. Add broth, increase heat to high, and bring just to a boil. Reduce heat to medium-low and simmer until zucchini is tender, 15 to 20 minutes.

For the basil cream: While soup is cooking, whisk together sour cream, basil, lemon juice, and a pinch of salt and pepper in a small bowl; set aside.

Purée soup in a blender or food processor, in batches if necessary, until smooth, or use a hand blender. Divide among 4 bowls, top with 1 tablespoon of basil cream, and serve.

Makes 4 (1-cup) servings

NUTRITION AT A GLANCE

Per serving: 120 calories, 9 g fat, 2 g saturated fat, 3 g protein, 10 g carbohydrate, 2 g fiber, 380 mg sodium

MAKE-AHEAD: Both the soup and the basil cream can be made up to 1 day in advance; refrigerate in separate covered containers until ready to use. If the cream separates, whisk again just before serving.

Fresh Crab Salad

PREP TIME: 25 minutes

Succulent and sweet, fresh crab makes any occasion elegant. Best when fussed with as little as possible, it gets a light accent here from chives, lemon, and black pepper. As with all fish and shellfish, crab should be purchased from a reputable purveyor, close to the date you intend to use it, and be kept well chilled until ready to use.

¼ pound fresh lump crabmeat (½ cup)

1 celery stalk, minced

2 tablespoons thinly sliced fresh basil

1 tablespoon fresh lemon juice

1 tablespoon finely chopped fresh chives

1½ teaspoons extra-virgin olive oil

Salt and freshly ground black pepper

4 medium Boston lettuce leaves

Place crabmeat in a medium bowl; pick through crabmeat and discard any cartilage. Add celery, basil, lemon juice, chives, oil, and a pinch of salt and pepper; stir gently to combine.

Place lettuce leaves on a cutting board; trim white base ends and discard. Spoon ¼ cup crab mixture onto the center of each leaf. Transfer to plates and serve.

Makes 4 (¼-cup) servings

NUTRITION AT A GLANCE
Per serving: 45 calories, 2 g fat, 0 g saturated fat, 6 g protein, 1 g carbohydrate, 0 g fiber, 170 mg sodium

MAKE-AHEAD: Crab mixture can be made up to 1 day ahead and refrigerated in a covered container until ready to use. Serve chilled or at room temperature.

Couscous with Toasted Pistachios

PREP TIME: 10 minutes   **COOK TIME:** 20 minutes

Buttery and slightly sweet, toasted pistachios team up well with couscous in this delicious side dish. The nuts also add significant nutritional value, as they are rich in fiber, thiamin, vitamin E, and iron.

⅓ cup shelled, unsalted pistachio nuts

1 tablespoon extra-virgin olive oil

½ cup minced red onion

1¼ cups whole-wheat couscous

1¾ cups boiling water

1 tablespoon fresh lemon juice

¼ teaspoon salt

Freshly ground black pepper

Heat oven to 275°F. Spread pistachios on a baking sheet and bake until fragrant and lightly toasted, about 8 minutes. Transfer nuts to a cutting board to cool. When cool, roughly chop nuts and set aside.

Heat oil in a medium nonstick saucepan over medium-high heat. Add onion, reduce heat to low, and cook until softened, about 4 minutes. Add couscous, stir to combine, and remove from heat.

Pour the boiling water over couscous, stir, cover, and let steam for 7 minutes. Remove cover and fluff couscous with a fork. Stir in pistachios, lemon juice, and salt. Season generously with pepper and serve hot.

Makes 6 (½-cup) servings

NUTRITION AT A GLANCE
Per serving: 150 calories, 6 g fat, 0.5 g saturated fat, 5 g protein, 22 g carbohydrate, 4 g fiber, 100 mg sodium

MAKE-AHEAD: Just the couscous can be prepared up to 1 day in advance and refrigerated in a covered container. Or it can be frozen for up to 1 month. Add pistachios, lemon juice, and seasonings just before serving and gently heat in a microwave or warm oven.

Broiled Halibut with Lemon and Dill

PREP TIME: 10 minutes   **COOK TIME:** 15 minutes

This simple-as-can-be fish dish is lovely and a real palate pleaser. The lemons become browned and slightly caramelized and should be served with the fish, rind and all.

2 small lemons, sliced into 16 thin slices

2 tablespoons chopped fresh dill

4 (6-ounce) pieces halibut fillet, about 1 inch thick

Salt and freshly ground black pepper

1 tablespoon extra-virgin olive oil

Dill sprigs for garnish (optional)

Heat oven to broil.

Line a broiler pan with foil. Lay 2 lemon slices vertically on the pan, just barely overlapping. Repeat to make three more pairs, placing pairs 1½ inches apart. Sprinkle the lemon slices evenly with 1 tablespoon of the chopped dill.

Pat fish dry, lightly season with salt and pepper, and place over lemon slices. Drizzle with oil and sprinkle fish evenly with remaining 1 tablespoon dill. Top each piece of fish with 2 barely overlapping lemon slices.

Broil fish until cooked through, 10 to 12 minutes. Serve hot, garnished with dill sprigs, if using.

Makes 4 (6-ounce) servings

NUTRITION AT A GLANCE
Per serving: 220 calories, 7 g fat, 1 g saturated fat, 35 g protein, 2 g carbohydrate, 0 g fiber, 95 mg sodium

Broccolini with Warm Sun-Dried Tomato Vinaigrette

PREP TIME: 15 minutes   **COOK TIME:** 15 minutes

Sun-dried tomatoes are common in pastas, salads, and wraps but less often thought of as flavor enhancers for vegetable side dishes. Here they merge with broccolini to form an unexpected and extremely appealing combination. You can use regular broccoli if broccolini isn't available.

1   pound broccolini, stems separated

4   sun-dried tomatoes (packed in oil), chopped, plus 4 teaspoons of the oil

2   tablespoons minced red onion

2   garlic cloves, very thinly sliced

Salt

1   teaspoon red wine vinegar

Freshly ground black pepper

Fill a large skillet with 2 inches of water; cover and bring to a simmer. Add broccolini, cover, and return to a simmer. Uncover and cook until broccolini is crisp-tender, about 2 minutes. Drain in a colander and immediately run under cold water for 1 minute to stop cooking. Drain again and pat dry.

Wipe skillet dry. Add tomatoes and their 4 teaspoons oil, onion, garlic, and a pinch of salt; cover and cook over medium-low heat until onion and garlic are slightly softened, about 3 minutes.

Uncover, add broccolini, and toss to coat with tomato mixture. Increase heat to medium and cook, uncovered, until broccolini is warmed through, about 3 minutes. Add vinegar and salt and pepper to taste; toss to coat. Serve warm.

Makes 4 servings

NUTRITION AT A GLANCE
Per serving: 70 calories, 5 g fat, 1 g saturated fat, 3 g protein, 6 g carbohydrate, 3 g fiber, 30 mg sodium

MAKE-AHEAD: Broccolini can be cooked to crisp-tender up to 1 day in advance; pat dry and store in a covered container until ready to complete the recipe.

Lemon-Thyme Ices

PREP TIME: 15 minutes   **FREEZING TIME:** 2 hours

This pretty dessert makes a lovely ending to a wonderful celebration of Mom. Reminiscent of an Italian lemon ice, it is updated here with a hint of fresh thyme. If you prefer a less tart finale to the meal, add a little more sugar substitute.

> 3 leafy fresh thyme sprigs, plus 4 extra sprigs for garnish
>
> ½ cup granular sugar substitute
>
> 2 cups boiling water
>
> 1 cup fresh lemon juice (from 5 to 6 lemons)
>
> 1 tablespoon grated lemon zest
>
>   Salt

Place thyme sprigs and sugar substitute in a medium metal bowl. Pour boiling water over them and stir to dissolve sugar substitute. Steep for 3 minutes, then remove thyme sprigs and discard then.

Place bowl in freezer until mixture is cool, about 10 minutes. Remove from freezer and whisk in lemon juice, zest, and a pinch of salt. Pour into 2 standard ice cube trays, filling each ice cube compartment to just below the top (you will fill 1 tray and half of a second one).

Freeze until mostly frozen through, 1½ to 2 hours. Place cubes in a food processor or blender and pulse very briefly, just until the ice becomes granular. (Don't overprocess, or the drink will be a liquid.)

Transfer ice to dessert bowls, garnish with thyme sprig tops, and serve immediately.

Makes 4 (generous ½-cup) servings

NUTRITION AT A GLANCE
Per serving: 30 calories, 0 g fat, 0 g saturated fat, 0 g protein, 9 g carbohydrate, 0 g fiber, 0 mg sodium

FOURTH OF JULY REVEL

FOR 10 GUESTS

A warm summer day, a bright blue sky, and a group of friends and relatives are the basics for a great Fourth of July celebration. Mix in the scent of grilling burgers, a festive parade, the waving of flags, and the flash, bang, and boom of sparkling fireworks and you've got a spirited day that everyone will remember.

This party's picnic-table fare includes loads of summer's best vegetables and herbs. You can begin the meal with a beautiful, juicy tomato salad tossed with olive oil and basil or serve the salad right along with the burgers. A second, heartier pasta salad is enhanced with fresh snow peas and thyme. And asparagus and plump portobellos are grilled to perfection.

The stars will come out before dark in the form of rich almond cookies, which kids will love for their shape and adults for their grown-up nutty flavor. Your festive decor can include napkins, plates, and aprons in—of course—red, white, and blue.

◄A Fourth of July picnic wouldn't be complete without grilled burgers and plenty of summery side dishes. A red, white, and blue dessert is a must.

MENU

Fresh Tomato Salad

Firecracker Cheddar Burgers

Pasta and Snow Pea Salad

Grilled Asparagus and Portobello Mushrooms

Star-Spangled Berries

Almond Star Cookies

Strawberry-Limeade Sparklers

Holiday Game Plan

Up to 1 month before: Make and freeze cookie dough.

Up to 2 days before: Thaw cookie dough.

Up to 1 day before: Prepare pasta and pasta ingredients; bake cookies; toast pita chips; prepare ricotta for berries; make strawberry-lime sparkler base.

Day of: Assemble pasta salad and berry dish; make tomato salad; prepare and grill hamburgers and grilled vegetables; make sparklers.

Fresh Tomato Salad

PREP TIME: 10 minutes

The vivid red color and incomparably juicy taste of a ripe summer tomato simply can't be beat. Here, in this easy salad, aromatic basil leaves, a bit of lemon zest, and some good-quality olive oil are all it takes for this favorite fruit to shine. If you live near a farmers' market, try using a variety of heirloom tomatoes—the colors, flavors, shapes, and sizes are unique and very special.

- 2 pounds ripe tomatoes, cut into thin wedges
- 1 bunch fresh basil, leaves picked and thinly sliced
- 3 tablespoons extra-virgin olive oil
- 1½ teaspoons finely grated lemon zest

  Salt and freshly ground black pepper

Combine tomatoes, basil, oil, and zest in a serving bowl. Season to taste with salt and pepper, and serve.

Makes 10 (generous ½-cup) servings

NUTRITION AT A GLANCE
Per serving: 50 calories, 4.5 g fat, 0.5 g saturated fat, 1 g protein, 4 g carbohydrate, 1 g fiber, 0 mg sodium

TIP **Storing tomatoes:** Store tomatoes stem side down at room temperature, away from direct sunlight and heat. Do not refrigerate tomatoes, as cold temperatures will rob them of flavor and create a mealy texture.

Firecracker Cheddar Burgers

PREP TIME: 25 minutes   **COOK TIME:** 10 minutes

A bit of cayenne pepper gives these burgers a subtle kick of heat. If you're expecting kids, leave some of the meat unseasoned. And, if you know you have a hungry crowd coming, double the recipe. Phase 1 dieters can enjoy the burger without the bun.

- ¼ cup Dijon mustard
- ⅓ cup finely chopped red onion
- 3 garlic cloves, minced
- 2 large egg yolks
- ½ teaspoon cayenne pepper
- 2½ pounds lean ground beef
- 1 tablespoon canola oil, for grill
- 5 ounces reduced-fat cheddar cheese, shredded
- 10 multigrain buns

Whisk together mustard, onion, garlic, egg yolks, and cayenne in a large bowl. Add beef and stir until combined. Form mixture into 10 patties, about ¾ inch thick.

Lightly oil a grill or grill pan and heat to medium-high. Cook burgers 4 to 5 minutes per side for medium-rare, sprinkling cheese evenly over burgers for the last 2 minutes of cooking. Serve burgers on lightly grilled buns.

Makes 10 servings

NUTRITION AT A GLANCE
Per serving (with bun): 340 calories, 12 g fat, 4 g saturated fat, 33 g protein, 24 g carbohydrate, 3 g fiber, 520 mg sodium

Per serving (without bun): 210 calories, 10 g fat, 3.5 g saturated fat, 29 g protein, 2 g carbohydrate, 0 g fiber, 320 mg sodium

MAKE-AHEAD: Beef mixture can be formed into patties the morning of the party. Keep well wrapped and refrigerated until ready to cook.

Pasta and Snow Pea Salad

PREP TIME: 20 minutes   **COOK TIME:** 35 minutes

Any small-shaped pasta will work well in this recipe. If you can't find fusilli, try penne or radiatore.

¼ cup plus 2 tablespoons extra-virgin olive oil

3 large red onions, coarsely chopped

10 garlic cloves, smashed and peeled

Salt

1½ pounds snow peas, trimmed

1 pound whole-wheat fusilli pasta

⅓ cup red wine vinegar

3 tablespoons sliced fresh basil leaves

1 tablespoon fresh thyme leaves

Freshly ground black pepper

Heat 2 tablespoons of the oil in a large nonstick skillet over medium heat. Add onions, garlic, and a pinch of salt. Reduce heat to low, cover, and cook for 10 minutes, stirring once. Uncover and continue cooking until onions are very tender and lightly caramelized, 20 to 25 minutes more.

Meanwhile, bring a large pot of lightly salted water to a boil. Add snow peas to boiling water and cook 1 minute. Keeping water at a boil, carefully use a slotted spoon or mesh strainer to transfer peas to a colander. Immediately run under very cold water for 1 minute to stop cooking. Rinse again and pat dry; cut peas in half on the bias.

In the boiling water you used for the peas, cook the pasta according to package directions to al dente. Drain pasta (do not rinse) and return to the pot off the heat; cover and keep warm.

When the onion mixture is ready, add it to the pasta along with the peas, remaining ¼ cup oil, vinegar, basil, thyme, and salt and pepper to taste. Serve warm or at room temperature.

Makes 16 (1-cup) servings

NUTRITION AT A GLANCE
Per serving: 180 calories, 6 g fat, 1 g saturated fat, 5 g protein, 28 g carbohydrate, 4 g fiber, 10 mg sodium

MAKE-AHEAD: Pasta can be cooked, tossed with the onion mixture, and refrigerated in a covered container up to 1 day in advance. Peas can also be cooked, patted dry, sliced, and refrigerated in a covered container up to 1 day ahead. Bring pasta and peas to room temperature and toss with vinegar, herbs, and seasonings just before serving.

Grilled Asparagus and Portobello Mushrooms

PREP TIME: 10 minutes   **COOK TIME:** 25 minutes

Balsamic vinegar adds a touch of sweetness to these easy veggies. For an outside grill, use a grill topper so the asparagus don't fall through the grate. Inside, grill in batches, if necessary.

2	tablespoons canola oil
10	large portobello mushrooms, stems removed
2	pounds asparagus, tough ends trimmed
3	tablespoons balsamic vinegar
	Salt and freshly ground black pepper

Heat a grill or grill pan to medium-high; brush lightly with some of the oil. Grill mushrooms and asparagus, in batches if necessary, until cooked through, brushing lightly with oil just after placing on the grill and turning once or twice. Mushrooms will take 5 to 7 minutes per side, depending on size and thickness; asparagus will take 3 to 5 minutes per side.

Remove vegetables from grill. Slice mushrooms into ¾-inch-thick slices and transfer to a medium bowl. Add vinegar and salt and pepper to taste; toss to coat. Transfer mushrooms to the center of a large serving platter. Place asparagus around mushrooms and season lightly with salt and pepper. Serve warm.

Makes 10 servings

NUTRITION AT A GLANCE
Per serving: 70 calories, 3 g fat, 0 g saturated fat, 4 g protein, 9 g carbohydrate, 3 g fiber, 5 mg sodium

Star-Spangled Berries

PREP TIME: 15 minutes

Nothing reflects the spirit of America's birthday bash like the colors red, white, and blue. Bring out this refreshing dessert just in time for the fireworks!

2   (16-ounce) containers strawberries, hulled

2   pints blueberries

4   tablespoons granular sugar substitute

1   tablespoon plus 2 teaspoons fresh lemon juice

2   cups part-skim ricotta cheese

2   teaspoons vanilla extract

Halve or quarter strawberries, depending on size. Combine strawberries, blueberries, 1 tablespoon of the sugar substitute, and 1 tablespoon of the lemon juice in a large bowl.

Process ricotta, remaining 3 tablespoons sugar substitute, remaining 2 teaspoons lemon juice, and vanilla in a blender or food processor until ricotta is smooth, about 2 minutes.

Spread ricotta mixture evenly on the bottom of a wide, shallow serving bowl or 4-quart rectangular serving dish. Top evenly with the berries and serve.

Makes 10 (generous 1-cup) servings

NUTRITION AT A GLANCE
Per serving: 140 calories, 4.5 g fat, 2.5 g saturated fat, 7 g protein, 19 g carbohydrate, 3 g fiber, 65 mg sodium

MAKE-AHEAD: Prepare ricotta mixture up to 1 day ahead and refrigerate in a covered container until ready to use. Don't hull or wash the strawberries until just before you are ready to slice them.

Almond Star Cookies

PREP TIME: 15 minutes   **CHILL TIME:** 1 to 2 hours   **COOK TIME:** 30 minutes

Ground nuts and whole-grain flour add texture and sophisticated flavor to these sweet and festive cookie stars. Use a variety of star cutters if you have them to create a more dramatic effect. The dough is also ideal for Christmas cookies.

1 cup whole almonds

1 cup whole-grain pastry flour

1 cup unbleached all-purpose flour

⅓ cup granular sugar substitute

Salt

1 cup trans-fat-free margarine, cut into small pieces and refrigerated

½ teaspoon finely grated lemon zest

½ teaspoon vanilla extract

¼ teaspoon almond extract

Heat oven to 275°F. Spread almonds on a baking sheet and toast until fragrant and lightly golden, about 10 minutes. Remove from oven, transfer to a plate, and cool completely.

Pulse almonds, whole-grain and all-purpose flours, sugar substitute, and a pinch of salt in a food processor until nuts are finely ground. Add margarine and pulse until margarine is incorporated. Add zest and vanilla and almond extracts; pulse until dough just begins to come together.

Remove dough from processor to a work surface. Knead once or twice, divide in half, and form into 2 flat disks. Wrap disks and freeze for 1 hour or refrigerate for at least 2 hours.

Heat oven to 325°F. Lightly coat 2 baking sheets with cooking spray.

Roll out 1 disk of dough between 2 sheets of wax paper to ⅛ inch thick. Cut as many stars as possible, carefully transferring them to the baking sheets as you go. (Use a butter knife or small spatula to make transferring cut cookie dough from wax paper to baking sheets easier.) Reroll and cut the scraps. (If the dough becomes too soft while cutting, wrap and chill again until firm.) Repeat with the second disk.

Bake cookies until lightly golden on edges and bottoms, rotating sheets once halfway through, 16 to 18 minutes. Let cool on sheets for 2 to 3 minutes before transferring with a spatula to wire racks to cool completely.

Makes 4 dozen (2-inch) stars or 3 dozen (3-inch) stars

NUTRITION AT A GLANCE
Per 2-inch cookie: 70 calories, 4.5 g fat, 1 g saturated fat, 1 g protein, 5 g carbohydrate, 1 g fiber, 30 mg sodium
Per 3-inch cookie: 90 calories, 6 g fat, 1.5 g saturated fat, 2 g protein, 6 g carbohydrate, 1 g fiber, 40 mg sodium

MAKE-AHEAD: Dough can be frozen in freezer-proof resealable plastic bags up to 1 month in advance. Cookies can be baked up to 1 day in advance and stored in an airtight container at room temperature or in the refrigerator.

PHASE 2

Strawberry-Limeade Sparklers

PREP TIME: 15 minutes

This thirst-quenching and fun twist on lemonade can be made with lemon juice in place of the lime juice or with a mixture of both.

1 (10-ounce) package frozen strawberries, thawed, with juices

¼ cup fresh lime juice

2 tablespoons granular sugar substitute

1 (2-liter) bottle seltzer water

Ice cubes

2 limes, cut into 5 thin slices each

Purée strawberries and their juices, lime juice, and sugar substitute in a blender. For each drink, place 2 tablespoons plus 1 teaspoon strawberry mixture in an 8-ounce glass. Add ¾ cup seltzer water and stir. Add ice cubes, garnish with a lime slice, and serve.

Makes 10 (1-cup) drinks

NUTRITION AT A GLANCE
Per drink: 15 calories, 0 g fat, 0 g saturated fat, 0 g protein, 3 g carbohydrate, 0 g fiber, 0 mg sodium

MAKE-AHEAD: Strawberry-lime drink base can be made up to 1 day in advance and refrigerated in a covered container until ready to use. Add seltzer water to drinks individually, just before serving.

THANKSGIVING

FOR 8 GUESTS

Thanksgiving. The very mention of the word instantly conjures up a host of wonderful images: beloved friends and family gathered together; a golden turkey waiting to be carved; bowls overflowing with the bounty of the season.

On the South Beach Diet, there's no skimping when it comes to America's favorite food holiday. Classic trimmings such as hearty pear and sausage stuffing, fruity cranberry-orange compote, and warm, garlicky green beans accompany the tender and juicy bird. And for the grand finale, there's creamy pumpkin pie.

Decor for this occasion can be as lush as the meal or as simple as a centerpiece of dried flowers and berry stems. With a box of crayons and a pile of blank index cards, kids can make a colorful autumn leaf or turkey place cards.

Because Thanksgiving is a time to reflect on your good fortune, take a moment to acknowledge the most important—your health! Applaud your daily efforts to improve your well-being and then . . . get ready to celebrate with this satisfying holiday meal.

◀ *This South Beach Diet–friendly Thanksgiving dinner features roast turkey with all the traditional trimmings.*

MENU

Roast Turkey with Fresh Herbs

Pan Juice "Gravy"

Turkey Sausage and Pear Stuffing

Cranberry-Orange Compote

*Green Beans
with Garlic and Lemon*

Cider-Roasted Sweet Potatoes

Cauliflower Mash

Pumpkin Pie

Turkey Chili (for leftover turkey)

Holiday Game Plan

Up to 1 month before: Order a fresh turkey, if using.

Up to 1 week before: Make compote.

Up to 4 days before: Thaw frozen turkey, if using, in refrigerator.

Up to 1 day before: Make stuffing and cauliflower; blanch beans; make pie filling.

Day of: Assemble and bake pie; roast turkey and sweet potatoes; make gravy; finish beans; heat stuffing and cauliflower while turkey is resting.

Roast Turkey with Fresh Herbs

PREP TIME: 15 minutes   COOK TIME: 3½ hours

As a South Beach Dieter, be sure to choose the tasty and moist white meat, and don't forget to remove the skin from your portion before eating.

- 1 12- to 14-pound turkey
- ½ teaspoon salt
- ½ teaspoon freshly ground black pepper
- 1 small orange, apple, and/or onion, halved
- 1 tablespoon chopped fresh parsley
- 1 tablespoon chopped fresh thyme leaves
- 3 tablespoons extra-virgin olive oil
- 3 tablespoons dry white wine or lower-sodium chicken broth

Position rack in the lower third of oven and heat oven to 450°F.

Rinse turkey under cold water and pat dry with paper towels. Sprinkle inside of bird with ¼ teaspoon of the salt and ¼ teaspoon of the pepper. Insert orange, apple, and/or onion halves into cavity of bird. Tuck wings under and tie legs together with kitchen twine. Place turkey on a rack in a roasting pan.

Combine remaining ¼ teaspoon salt, ¼ teaspoon pepper, parsley, and thyme in a small bowl. Slide your hand under skin of turkey breast to loosen skin. Rub turkey breast under skin with 1 tablespoon of the oil. Spread herb mixture over breast and press skin back down on top.

Transfer turkey to oven and roast for 30 minutes. Remove from oven, baste with 1 tablespoon of the remaining oil and 1 tablespoon of the wine. Reduce oven temperature to 350°F and roast for 30 minutes more; baste with the remaining 1 tablespoon oil and remaining 2 tablespoons wine.

Continue to roast, basting every 30 minutes with accumulated pan juices, until a meat thermometer reads 180°F when inserted into the thickest part of the thigh, 1½ to 2 hours more. Remove turkey from oven, cover loosely with foil, and allow bird to rest for 20 minutes before carving. Remove and discard orange halves, carve bird, and serve.

Makes 8 (6-ounce) servings, with leftovers

NUTRITION AT A GLANCE
Per serving (without skin): 250 calories, 8 g fat, 1.5 g saturated fat, 38 g protein, 0 g carbohydrate, 0 g fiber, 260 mg sodium

Pan Juice "Gravy"

PREP TIME: 5 minutes   **COOK TIME:** 20 minutes

This "jus"-style gravy, made without flour or cornstarch, is thickened naturally by reducing and concentrating the turkey juices. After the bird is carved and placed on a serving platter, add the juices from the cutting board to the gravy for extra richness.

- 1   cup dry white wine
- 2   cups lower-sodium chicken broth

After turkey has roasted, pour juices from the pan into a glass measuring cup or a fat separator; set aside. Place the roasting pan on the stove over medium-high heat. Add wine to the pan and, using a wooden spoon, scrape any browned bits of turkey from the bottom of the pan. Add broth, bring to a simmer, and cook until reduced by half, about 5 minutes.

Meanwhile, skim off any fat that has accumulated on top of the reserved pan juices (you should have about 2 cups of juices). Add juices to the roasting pan along with any additional juices that have accumulated on the carving board. Bring to a simmer and cook until reduced by half, stirring occasionally. Serve warm.

Makes 8 (¼-cup) servings

NUTRITION AT A GLANCE
Per serving: 25 calories, 1 g fat, 0 g saturated fat, 1 g protein, 1 g carbohydrate, 0 g fiber, 105 mg sodium

TIP **Easy turkey carving:** A sharp knife is the key to easy carving and smooth cuts that won't shred the meat. After the turkey has rested, remove the turkey legs and set aside. Then, just above the wing, make a long, deep horizontal cut. Finally, slice down vertically from the top of the breast to the initial cut. Easy and beautiful!

Turkey Sausage and Pear Stuffing

PREP TIME: 20 minutes   COOK TIME: 45 minutes

If you prefer, use a multigrain bread with lots of grains and seeds to add extra texture and heartiness to this healthy stuffing. Bartlett or Anjou pears are good substitutes for Bosc.

3 teaspoons extra-virgin olive oil, plus extra for baking dish

1 (¾-pound) loaf whole-grain bread, cut into cubes (4 cups)

1 pound sweet Italian-style turkey sausage

½ cup lower-sodium chicken broth

4 celery stalks, coarsely chopped

1 medium onion, coarsely chopped

1 Bosc pear, coarsely chopped

1 tablespoon chopped fresh sage

1 large egg, lightly beaten

¼ cup chopped fresh parsley

¼ teaspoon salt

¼ teaspoon freshly ground black pepper

Heat oven to 350°F. Lightly oil a 9- by 13-inch baking dish. Place bread cubes in a large bowl.

Remove sausage from the casings and break into ½-inch pieces. Heat 1 teaspoon of the oil in a large skillet over medium-high heat. Add sausage and cook until browned, about 3 minutes. Transfer to the bowl with bread cubes.

Return the skillet to the heat. Add 2 tablespoons of the broth and, using a wooden spoon, scrape any browned bits of sausage from the bottom of the skillet. Add the remaining 2 teaspoons oil, celery, and onion; cook until softened, about 6 minutes. Add pear and sage; cook 2 minutes more.

Transfer vegetable mixture to the bowl with the bread and sausage. Add egg and stir to combine. Add remaining broth, parsley, salt, and pepper; mix well. Spread stuffing evenly in baking dish. Bake until top is crispy and stuffing is heated through, about 30 minutes.

Makes 12 cups

NUTRITION AT A GLANCE

Per ½ cup: 80 calories, 2 g fat, 0.5 g saturated fat, 6 g protein, 10 g carbohydrate, 2 g fiber, 125 mg sodium

MAKE-AHEAD: Stuffing can be made up to 1 day in advance; store in a covered container in the refrigerator. Reheat, covered, in a microwave or 325°F oven before serving.

Cranberry-Orange Compote

PREP TIME: 5 minutes   **COOK TIME:** 10 minutes

This classic jewel-colored fruit sauce is the perfect foil for turkey meat and makes a flavorful condiment for the next day's sandwiches (you might want to double this recipe to ensure leftovers). Low in calories, cranberries are also a good source of vitamin C. If you like a sweeter compote, add a little more sugar substitute.

> 2 cups fresh or frozen cranberries
>
> 1 tablespoon grated orange zest
>
> ⅛ teaspoon ground cinnamon
>
> 1 cup water
>
> ½ cup granular sugar substitute

Place cranberries, zest, cinnamon, and water in a medium saucepan over medium heat; stir to combine. Bring to a simmer and cook, stirring occasionally, until berries have popped and compote has thickened, about 10 minutes. Remove from heat and stir in sugar substitute to taste. Serve at room temperature.

Makes 8 (3-tablespoon) servings

NUTRITION AT A GLANCE
Per serving: 20 calories, 0 g fat, 0 g saturated fat, 0 g protein, 5 g carbohydrate, 1 g fiber, 0 mg sodium

MAKE-AHEAD: Compote can be made up to 1 week in advance and refrigerated in a covered container. Bring to room temperature before serving.

Green Beans with Garlic and Lemon

PREP TIME: 15 minutes   COOK TIME: 5 minutes

Green beans bring lovely color to the Thanksgiving table. Look for the long, skinny French beans called haricots verts. They're very tender and extra special.

1   pound green beans, trimmed

1   tablespoon extra-virgin olive oil

3   garlic cloves, minced

2   teaspoons grated lemon zest

1   tablespoon fresh lemon juice

Salt and freshly ground black pepper

Bring a medium saucepan of salted water to a boil. Add beans, return to a boil, and cook until crisp-tender, about 2 minutes. Drain in a colander and rinse under very cold water to stop cooking. Drain again and pat dry.

Heat oil in a large nonstick skillet. Add garlic and cook until softened, about 1 minute. Add beans and zest; cook, stirring occasionally, until beans are warmed through, about 2 minutes. Stir in lemon juice and season to taste with salt and pepper. Serve warm or at room temperature.

Makes 8 servings

NUTRITION AT A GLANCE
Per serving: 50 calories, 2 g fat, 0.5 g saturated fat, 1 g protein, 7 g carbohydrate, 4 g fiber, 0 mg sodium

MAKE-AHEAD: Beans can be blanched up to a day in advance.

Cider-Roasted Sweet Potatoes

PREP TIME: 10 minutes   COOK TIME: 30 minutes

The tasty skin of sweet potatoes offers abundant fiber, and the flesh supplies a hearty dose of vitamins B_6 and C, as well as potassium and iron. Remember that cider is drizzled on for flavor here; save drinking a full glass of cider for Phase 3.

6   medium sweet potatoes (about 3 pounds), sliced into 8 wedges each

1   tablespoon extra-virgin olive oil

½   teaspoon ground cinnamon

½   teaspoon salt

¼   teaspoon freshly ground black pepper

⅓   cup unsweetened apple cider

Heat oven to 400°F. Toss together potato slices, oil, cinnamon, salt, and pepper in a large bowl. Transfer to a large baking dish and drizzle with cider. Roast until lightly browned and cooked through, about 30 minutes.

Makes 8 servings

NUTRITION AT A GLANCE

Per serving: 130 calories, 2.5 g fat, 0 g saturated fat, 2 g protein, 25 g carbohydrate, 3 g fiber, 180 mg sodium

PHASE 1

Cauliflower Mash

PREP TIME: 5 minutes   COOK TIME: 15 minutes

Other South Beach Diet cookbooks have featured a mashed cauliflower recipe that has been such a hit, so we couldn't resist creating a new variation for Thanksgiving.

1½ pounds cauliflower, cut into large florets (about 8 cups)

3 garlic cloves

2 (14-ounce) cans lower-sodium chicken broth

Salt and freshly ground black pepper

2 tablespoons chopped fresh chives

Combine cauliflower, garlic, and broth in a large saucepan. If cauliflower is not completely covered by the broth, add water until just covered. Bring to a boil, reduce heat to medium-low, and simmer until cauliflower is tender, about 12 minutes.

Reserve 2 tablespoons of the cooking liquid and drain cauliflower. Transfer cauliflower and garlic to the bowl of a food processor, and process until smooth, pulsing in 1 or 2 tablespoons of the reserved broth, if necessary, to moisten the mixture. Season with salt and pepper to taste. Just before serving, stir in chives. Serve warm.

Makes 8 (½-cup) servings

NUTRITION AT A GLANCE

Per serving: 40 calories, 0.5 g fat, 0 g saturated fat, 4 g protein, 6 g carbohydrate, 2 g fiber, 55 mg sodium

MAKE-AHEAD: Recipe can be made up to 1 day in advance; refrigerate in a covered container and reheat in a microwave or 325°F oven before serving.

Pumpkin Pie

PREP TIME: 20 minutes   COOK TIME: 1 hour

Nothing makes Thanksgiving more complete than pumpkin pie. Redolent with warm spices, this creamy treat is enhanced with a delightfully crispy, light crust that tastes deceivingly buttery, though no butter is used. Whipped topping and chocolate shavings make a gorgeous and irresistible topping, if desired.

6   (9- by 14-inch) sheets whole-wheat phyllo dough, thawed

⅓   cup granular sugar substitute

1½   teaspoons ground cinnamon

½   teaspoon ground ginger

½   teaspoon salt

¼   teaspoon ground cloves

¼   teaspoon freshly grated nutmeg

1   (15-ounce) can pumpkin purée

4   large egg whites

1   large egg yolk

1   (12-ounce) can 2% evaporated milk

2   tablespoons sugar-free maple syrup

2   teaspoons vanilla extract

Light or fat-free whipped topping (optional)

Bittersweet chocolate for shavings (optional)

Position rack in middle of oven and heat oven to 350°F. Stack phyllo sheets on plastic wrap or wax paper; cover with a barely damp towel to prevent sheets from drying out.

Lightly coat a 9-inch pie plate with cooking spray. Lay 1 phyllo sheet in the pie plate. Coat sheet with cooking spray, making sure to spray edges. Repeat with remaining sheets, rotating each slightly in the pan to form a circle. Fold and crimp edges.

Place a piece of parchment or wax paper on top of crust. Weigh crust down with pie weights or dried beans and bake until edges are lightly golden, about 10 minutes. While crust is baking, combine sugar substitute, cinnamon, ginger, salt, cloves, and nutmeg in a medium bowl.

In a large bowl, with an electric mixer at medium speed, beat pumpkin purée, egg whites, and egg yolk until well blended. Slowly add milk, maple syrup, and vanilla, beating until blended. Add spice mixture and blend well.

Remove pie weights from crust. Pour filling into crust and bake until tester inserted in the center comes out clean, 45 to 50 minutes. Remove pie from oven and cool at room temperature to set. Just before serving, top each slice of pie with 1 to 2 tablespoons whipped topping and chocolate shavings, if desired.

Makes 8 servings

NUTRITION AT A GLANCE

Per serving: 130 calories, 2.5 g fat, 1 g saturated fat, 7 g protein, 19 g carbohydrate, 2 g fiber, 300 mg sodium

MAKE-AHEAD: Pie filling can be made up to 1 day in advance and refrigerated in a covered container until ready to use. Whisk well before filling pie shell.

Turkey Chili

PREP TIME: 10 minutes   **COOK TIME: 1 hour 10 minutes**

With leftover white-meat turkey and a few pantry items, you can whip up this one-pot favorite with little effort. It's best to make the chili within a couple of days after Thanksgiving so the turkey doesn't dry out. Salt-free pinto beans are available in supermarkets or health-food stores. Spice lovers can add a few dashes of hot pepper sauce to turn up the heat. Football anyone?

2   teaspoons extra-virgin olive oil

1   medium onion, chopped

2   garlic cloves, minced

2   teaspoons ground cumin

1   tablespoon chili powder

1   teaspoon dried oregano

¼   teaspoon ground cinnamon

1   (14.5-ounce) can lower-sodium chicken broth

1   (28-ounce) can unsalted chopped tomatoes

1   tablespoon unsalted tomato paste

1   pound cooked turkey breast, skin removed, cubed (about 3 cups)

1   (15-ounce) can unsalted pinto beans

Salt and freshly ground black pepper

2   scallions, thinly sliced (optional)

Heat oil in a large nonstick saucepan over medium heat. Add onion and cook until softened, about 5 minutes. Add garlic and cook 1 minute more. Stir in cumin, chili powder, oregano, and cinnamon. Add broth, tomatoes, and tomato paste. Simmer, partially covered, until slightly thickened, about 30 minutes.

Add turkey and beans and their liquid; simmer 30 minutes more, stirring occasionally. Season to taste with salt and pepper. Top with scallions, if desired. Serve hot or warm.

Makes 4 (1¾-cup) servings

NUTRITION AT A GLANCE
Per serving: 330 calories, 4 g fat, 0.5 g saturated fat, 45 g protein, 28 g carbohydrate, 8 g fiber, 390 mg sodium

MAKE-AHEAD: Chili can be frozen for up to 1 month.

Great Turkey Leftover Ideas

Part of the fun of Thanksgiving is having lots of leftover turkey to eat over the weekend. In addition to our Turkey Chili (opposite), here are some great ideas (and even one for breakfast!). All of the recipes serve two.

Ginger Turkey Stir-Fry (Phase 1): Stir together 1 tablespoon canola oil, 2 chopped scallions, 2 minced garlic cloves, ¼ teaspoon red pepper flakes, and 2 teaspoons minced ginger in a medium bowl. Add 2 cups cubed skinless white turkey meat and stir to coat; set aside for 10 minutes. Heat a large skillet over medium-high heat. Add turkey mixture and cook 1 to 2 minutes, stirring constantly. Add 2 cups small broccoli florets, ½ cup halved snow peas, 1 teaspoon toasted sesame oil, and 2 teaspoons low-sodium soy sauce. Cook 2 to 3 minutes more, stirring constantly. Serve hot.

Turkey Pasta Diablo (Phase 2): Cook 4 ounces whole-wheat spaghetti according to the package directions. Meanwhile, heat 1 tablespoon extra-virgin olive oil in a medium saucepan over medium heat. Add 1 chopped small onion, 2 minced garlic cloves, ½ teaspoon dried basil, and ⅛ teaspoon red pepper flakes. Reduce the heat to medium-low and cook until vegetables are softened, about 7 minutes. Add 1 cup finely diced skinless white turkey meat; stir and cook 2 to 3 minutes more. Add 1 cup canned chopped tomatoes and their juices; simmer sauce until heated through. Toss sauce with pasta and season to taste with salt and pepper. Serve hot with a light sprinkle of freshly grated Parmesan.

Curried Turkey Salad (Phase 1): Stir together ½ cup plain fat-free yogurt, ¼ cup mayonnaise, 1½ teaspoons curry powder, and ¼ teaspoon ground ginger in a medium bowl. Fold in 2 cups cubed skinless white turkey meat, 1 diced celery stalk, ½ diced cucumber, 2 tablespoons diced red onion, and 2 tablespoons chopped fresh herb, such as parsley or cilantro. Season to taste with salt and pepper. Serve over lightly dressed greens.

Mexican Turkey Scramble (Phase 1): Heat 2 teaspoons extra-virgin olive oil in a large nonstick skillet over medium heat. Add 2 thinly sliced scallions and cook for 1 minute. Add 1 cup finely diced skinless white turkey meat and 3 tablespoons fresh spicy salsa; cook 1 to 2 minutes more. Add 3 beaten eggs and, stirring constantly, cook until eggs are set. Top each serving with 2 avocado slices and serve with extra salsa, if desired.

HANUKKAH PARTY

FOR 8 GUESTS

Hanukkah celebrates the triumph of Judah Maccabee and his soldiers in their victory over the tyrant Antiochus more than 2,000 years ago. After a long, hard-fought battle, the Maccabees returned to Jerusalem to find their temple stripped by looters. They cleaned house, made repairs, and—having found just enough oil to light the menorah for one day—were surprised and blessed with the miracle of eight days of light.

Today the holiday is celebrated with the lighting of a candle on the menorah for each of the eight days, in memory of the miraculous oil. Naturally, part of the tradition is cooking foods in oil, including latkes—the potato pancakes that are loved by young and old. Crisp and delicious, they're made here with nutritious sweet potato and zucchini in place of white potato and cooked in healthy canola oil. A tender paprika-rubbed roast chicken, a hearty barley pilaf, and a lovely spinach salad with chickpeas all utilize olive oil and bring their own light to this joyful affair.

◀ *A perfectly roasted chicken serves as the centerpiece for this lovely Hanukkah dinner for friends and family.*

MENU

Tahini Dip with Veggies

Baby Spinach, Chickpea, and Feta Salad

Paprika Roast Chicken

Sweet Potato and Zucchini Latkes

Barley Pilaf with Roasted Cauliflower and Herbs

Cinnamon-Chocolate Mandelbrot

Holiday Game Plan

Up to 1 month before: Cook and freeze barley.

Up to 3 days before: Make mandelbrot.

Up to 2 days before: Make tahini dip; thaw barley and assemble pilaf.

Day of: Prepare veggies; make latkes; roast chicken; assemble salad.

Tahini Dip with Veggies

PREP TIME: 15 minutes

Popular in Middle Eastern cooking, tahini is a thick paste made from sesame seeds that's best known for its starring role in hummus and baba ghanoush. Mixed with low-fat yogurt and reduced-fat sour cream, tahini makes a creamy and nutty dip that pairs perfectly with crunchy vegetables.

1½ cups low-fat plain yogurt

½ cup reduced-fat sour cream

3 tablespoons chopped fresh chives

2 tablespoons tahini

2 teaspoons toasted sesame oil

¼ teaspoon salt

Assorted fresh vegetables, such as bell peppers, broccoli, cauliflower, celery, cucumber, endive, and blanched green beans

Combine yogurt, sour cream, chives, tahini, oil, and salt in a bowl; stir well. Serve dip with assorted vegetables of your choice.

Makes 2 cups

NUTRITION AT A GLANCE

Per tablespoon: 20 calories, 1.5 g fat, 0 g saturated fat, 1 g protein, 1 g carbohydrate, 0 g fiber, 30 mg sodium

MAKE-AHEAD: Dip can be made up to 2 days in advance (without chives) and refrigerated in a covered container. When ready to use, bring to room temperature, add chives, stir well, and serve.

Baby Spinach, Chickpea, and Feta Salad

PREP TIME: 10 minutes

Chickpeas are low in fat and high in fiber, iron, and other nutrients. They're as flavorful from the can as they are when cooked from a dried state.

8 ounces baby spinach leaves (about 11 cups)

1 (15-ounce) can chickpeas, rinsed and drained

2 ounces reduced-fat feta cheese, crumbled (½ cup)

2 tablespoons extra-virgin olive oil

1 tablespoon red wine vinegar

Salt and freshly ground black pepper

Combine spinach, chickpeas, and feta in a large bowl. Add oil and vinegar; toss to coat. Season to taste with salt and pepper and serve.

Makes 8 (1½-cup) servings

NUTRITION AT A GLANCE
Per serving: 90 calories, 5 g fat, 1 g saturated fat, 4 g protein, 9 g carbohydrate, 3 g fiber, 200 mg sodium

Paprika Roast Chicken

PREP TIME: 10 minutes **COOK TIME: 2 hours**

Thick onion slices add sumptuous flavor to this chicken, while also keeping it from sticking to the bottom of your roasting pan.

1 large onion, sliced into ½-inch-thick rounds	¾ teaspoon freshly ground black pepper
1 (8-pound) roasting chicken	1½ teaspoons paprika
¾ teaspoon salt	4 teaspoons extra-virgin olive oil

Heat oven to 400°F. Place onion slices in a single layer in a roasting pan. Rinse chicken under cold water and pat dry with paper towels. Sprinkle the inside cavity with ¼ teaspoon of the salt and ¼ teaspoon of the pepper

Place chicken on top of onion slices, tuck the wings under, and tie the legs together. Combine remaining ½ teaspoon salt, ½ teaspoon pepper, and paprika in a small bowl. Slide your hand under skin of chicken breast to loosen skin. Rub chicken breast under skin with 1 teaspoon of the oil and most of paprika mixture. Press skin back down. Rub outside of skin with 2 teaspoons of the remaining oil. Dust lightly with remaining paprika mixture.

Roast chicken for 30 minutes. Baste with remaining 1 teaspoon oil, then reduce oven temperature to 350°F. Continue to roast, basting every 30 minutes with accumulated pan juices, until a meat thermometer reads 180°F when placed into the thickest part of the thigh, about 1½ hours. Allow chicken to rest for 15 minutes before serving hot with onions, if desired.

Makes 12 (6-ounce) servings

NUTRITION AT A GLANCE
Per serving (without skin): 230 calories, 6 g fat, 1.5 g saturated fat, 40 g protein, 0 g carbohydrate, 0 g fiber, 280 mg sodium

Sweet Potato and Zucchini Latkes

PREP TIME: 10 minutes   **COOK TIME:** 10 minutes

Our twist on this Hanukkah favorite yields a delightfully crispy and slightly sweet pancake. Prepare the batter right before cooking to prevent excess liquid and soggy cakes; pour off any excess liquid while cooking, if necessary. These lacey latkes are delicate, so don't press down too hard on them once they are in the pan.

  1 medium zucchini (½ pound), ends trimmed

  1 large sweet potato (¾ pound), peeled

 ¼ cup minced onion

  1 large egg, lightly beaten

 ¼ teaspoon salt

 ⅛ teaspoon freshly ground black pepper

  3 tablespoons canola oil

     Unsweetened applesauce (optional)

Slice zucchini lengthwise and remove seeds. Coarsely grate zucchini and potato in a food processor or with a hand grater; transfer to a medium bowl. Add onion, egg, salt, and pepper; stir to combine.

Heat 1½ tablespoons of the oil in a large nonstick skillet over medium-high heat. Working in 2 batches, add zucchini mixture by heaping tablespoons to skillet, gently flattening with the back of the spoon as you go. Cook until the edges are golden, 1 to 2 minutes, then flip and cook until bottom is golden, about 1 minute more (adjust heat if necessary to prevent burning). Drain on paper towels. Repeat with remaining 1½ tablespoons oil and remaining zucchini mixture. Serve latkes hot with applesauce on the side, if desired.

Makes 24 (2-inch) latkes

NUTRITION AT A GLANCE
Per 2 latkes: 100 calories, 1 g fat, 0 g saturated fat, 4 g protein, 20 g carbohydrate, 4 g fiber, 220 mg sodium

MAKE-AHEAD: Latkes can be made up to 6 hours in advance and kept covered at room temperature. Reheat on a baking sheet (preferably dark bottomed) at 375°F until warmed through, about 5 minutes.

Barley Pilaf with Roasted Cauliflower and Herbs

PREP TIME: 10 minutes   **COOK TIME:** 50 minutes

The nutty flavor and toothsome texture of barley make it a wonderful side dish that's perfect for blending with fresh or dried herbs and roasted vegetables. Try adding roasted carrots and/or peppers along with (or instead of) the cauliflower.

> 3¾ cups vegetable broth
>
> 1½ cups barley
>
> 1 pound cauliflower, cut into small florets (about 8 cups)
>
> 4 tablespoons extra-virgin olive oil
>
> ½ teaspoon dried basil
>
> ½ teaspoon dried thyme
>
>   Salt and freshly ground black pepper
>
> ¼ cup chopped fresh parsley
>
> 4 scallions, green parts only, sliced
>
> 1 tablespoon red wine vinegar

Heat oven to 400°F.

Bring broth to a boil in a large saucepan. Add barley and stir. Cover, reduce to a simmer, and cook until water is absorbed and barley is tender, 40 to 45 minutes. Remove from the heat and allow to sit, covered, for 5 minutes.

While barley is cooking, toss cauliflower with 3 tablespoons of the oil, basil, and thyme in a large ovenproof casserole. Season lightly with salt and pepper. Roast cauliflower in oven, stirring every 10 minutes, until golden and tender, about 30 minutes.

Stir together cooked barley, roasted cauliflower, parsley, scallions, vinegar, and remaining 1 tablespoon oil in a large serving bowl. Season to taste with salt and pepper, and serve warm or at room temperature.

Makes 8 (¾-cup) servings

NUTRITION AT A GLANCE

Per serving: 220 calories, 8 g fat, 1 g saturated fat, 6 g protein, 31 g carbohydrate, 8 g fiber, 160 mg sodium

MAKE-AHEAD: Pilaf can be made up to 2 days in advance. Store in a covered container in the refrigerator and bring to room temperature before serving. Barley can be cooked by itself and frozen for up to 1 month; defrost in the refrigerator before using.

Cinnamon-Chocolate Mandelbrot

PREP TIME: 15 minutes   **COOK TIME:** 45 minutes (including cooling time)

These twice-baked cookies, a Hanukkah favorite, are similar to Italian biscotti.

½ cup whole almonds

½ cup trans-fat-free margarine, melted

¼ cup plus 2 tablespoons granular sugar substitute

¼ cup undiluted orange juice concentrate, thawed

2 large eggs

1 tablespoon grated orange zest

1 teaspoon vanilla extract

1 cup whole-grain pastry flour

1 cup unbleached all-purpose flour

2 teaspoons baking powder

4 teaspoons ground cinnamon

¼ teaspoon salt

¼ cup chopped bittersweet chocolate or chocolate chips

Heat oven to 350°F. Place almonds on a baking sheet and bake until fragrant and lightly toasted, about 8 minutes. Cool and coarsely chop.

Combine margarine, ¼ cup of the sugar substitute, orange juice concentrate, eggs, zest, and vanilla in a medium bowl.

In a large bowl, sift together whole-grain and all-purpose flours, baking powder, 2 teaspoons of the cinnamon, and salt. Stir in chopped almonds and chocolate. Make a well in the center of the dry ingredients. Add the wet ingredients and stir just to combine. Using your hands, knead the dough gently until it sticks together and forms a ball. Divide dough in half and shape each half into an 8-inch-long log. Place logs on a baking sheet and press each gently to flatten to 1-inch thickness. Bake logs for 20 minutes, remove from oven, and cool on a wire rack for 10 minutes. Meanwhile, combine remaining 2 tablespoons sugar substitute and 2 teaspoons cinnamon in a small bowl.

When logs are cool, use a serrated knife to cut each log crosswise into 12 pieces. Lay cookies flat on the baking sheet and sprinkle the tops evenly with the cinnamon mixture. Bake until cookies are lightly golden, about 12 minutes. Transfer to a wire rack to cool and serve.

Makes 2 dozen cookies

NUTRITION AT A GLANCE

Per cookie: 100 calories, 6 g fat, 1.5 g saturated fat, 3 g protein, 11 g carbohydrate, 1 g fiber, 60 mg sodium

MAKE-AHEAD: Mandelbrot can be made up to 3 days in advance. Store in a covered container.

CHRISTMAS EVE DINNER

FOR 8 GUESTS

Filled with joyous anticipation for the coming day, Christmas Eve is a time to delight in the company of those closest to you and enjoy one of the most sumptuous meals of the year. Greet guests at the door with our light cocoa eggnog and then lure them in to view the tree with the fragrant aroma of freshly baked spiced nuts.

Once at the table, the celebration continues with traditional and innovative yuletide foods, including tender roasted beef with a creamy, peppery horseradish sauce, barley with mushrooms prepared risotto-style, and a sweet purée of butternut squash. A green and red leaf salad tossed with an easy homemade champagne vinaigrette can be served after the meal and leads up to the perfect Christmas dessert: baked pears draped with sweet, melted chocolate and sprinkled with ruby red pomegranate seeds. Don't be surprised when no one wants to leave this jolly evening, even though Santa is on his way.

◄ *Hearty and healthy red wine makes the perfect accompaniment at this night-before-Christmas meal and takes the chill off a winter evening.*

MENU

Spiced Cocoa Eggnog

Holiday Spiced Nuts

Beef Tenderloin with Horseradish Sauce

Barley and Mushroom "Risotto"

Butternut Squash Purée

Red and Green Leaf Salad with Champagne Vinaigrette

Baked Pears with Chocolate Sauce and Pomegranate Seeds

Holiday Game Plan

Up to 3 days before: Make spiced nuts and risotto; seed pomegranate for pears.

Up to 1 day before: Make sauce for beef, squash, and salad dressing; bake pears.

Day of: Make eggnog; roast beef; assemble salad; heat risotto and squash; prepare chocolate mixture and assemble pears.

Spiced Cocoa Eggnog

PREP TIME: 10 minutes

This frothy new version of everyone's favorite yuletide beverage is sure to spread holiday cheer.

- 1 cup plus 2 tablespoons egg substitute
- 1 tablespoon granular sugar substitute
- 1½ (12-ounce) cans fat-free evaporated milk, chilled
- 2¼ cups fat-free half-and-half
- 2 tablespoons rum extract
- 1 tablespoon plus 1½ teaspoons vanilla extract
- 1 tablespoon unsweetened cocoa powder
- ½ teaspoon ground cinnamon
   Freshly grated nutmeg (optional)

In a large bowl, with an electric mixer at high speed, beat egg substitute and sugar substitute until light and frothy, about 3 minutes. With machine running, slowly pour in milk, half-and-half, and rum and vanilla extracts; beat to combine. Add cocoa and cinnamon; beat to combine.

Pour eggnog into cups, sprinkle each serving lightly with nutmeg, if using, and serve immediately.

Makes 12 (¾-cup) drinks

NUTRITION AT A GLANCE
Per drink: 70 calories, 0.5 g fat, 0 g saturated fat, 6 g protein, 8 g carbohydrate, 0 g fiber, 140 mg sodium

MAKE-AHEAD: Eggnog is best served immediately, as it's at its most frothy when just prepared. It can be made up to 1 day ahead but will lose some of its loft, so whip well with an electric hand mixer on high before serving.

Holiday Spiced Nuts

PREP TIME: 5 minutes   **COOK TIME:** 20 minutes

Although these nuts can be made up to 3 days in advance, they create a welcoming aroma for your guests when prepared just before the party begins. Remember that while nuts are high in protein and contain a host of beneficial nutrients, they're also high in calories; South Beach Dieters should stick to the recommended ¼-cup serving. For a spicier version, add an additional ¼ teaspoon of cayenne.

  1 large egg white

  2 teaspoons ground cinnamon

  ¾ teaspoon ground ginger

  ¼ teaspoon ground cloves

  ¼ teaspoon cayenne pepper

  2 cups unsalted nuts, such as roasted peanuts, walnuts, pecans, and/or almonds

  ⅛ teaspoon salt (optional)

Heat oven to 325°F. Line a baking sheet with parchment or foil.

Whisk egg white until frothy in a large bowl. Whisk in cinnamon, ginger, cloves, and cayenne. Add nuts and toss until well coated.

Spread nuts on baking sheet. Bake until nuts appear dry, about 20 minutes. Cool completely. Sprinkle with salt, if using, just before serving.

Makes 8 (¼-cup) servings

NUTRITION AT A GLANCE
Per serving: 170 calories, 16 g fat, 1.5 g saturated fat, 4 g protein, 4 g carbohydrate, 2 g fiber, 40 mg sodium

MAKE-AHEAD: Nuts can be made up to 3 days ahead and stored in an airtight container at room temperature. Do not refrigerate.

Beef Tenderloin with Horseradish Sauce

PREP TIME: 10 minutes   **COOK TIME:** 35 minutes   **RESTING TIME:** 15 minutes

This rich, savory roast is both elegant and festive. The peppery, cool sauce can easily be adjusted with the addition of more horseradish or mustard, if you like a more piquant version. Order your tenderloin already tied from the butcher, if possible. Or, to tie it yourself, fold the thin end of the tenderloin under and tie the roast in about 10 places so it is approximately the same thickness throughout. This ensures even cooking.

Tenderloin

- 1 (4-pound) whole beef tenderloin, tied
- 2 tablespoons coarsely ground black pepper
- 1 teaspoon dried rosemary, crushed
- ½ teaspoon salt
- 2 tablespoons extra-virgin olive oil

Sauce

- 1 (8-ounce) container reduced-fat sour cream
- 2 tablespoons prepared horseradish
- 1½ teaspoons red wine vinegar
- 1 teaspoon Dijon mustard
- ¼ teaspoon salt
- ⅛ teaspoon freshly ground black pepper

Heat oven to 450°F.

For the tenderloin: Place meat in a large baking pan. Combine pepper, rosemary, and salt in a small bowl. Rub meat all over with oil, then rub in seasonings.

Roast until meat thermometer measures 125°F for medium-rare, 30 to 35 minutes. Allow meat to rest for 15 minutes before slicing into ¼-inch-thick slices. Serve warm with horseradish sauce.

For the sauce: While meat is cooking, whisk together sour cream, horseradish, vinegar, mustard, salt, and pepper in a small bowl. Serve at room temperature with tenderloin.

Makes 8 (6-ounce) servings and 1 cup sauce

NUTRITION AT A GLANCE

Per serving (with 2 tablespoons sauce): 360 calories, 18 g fat, 7 g saturated fat, 45 g protein, 3 g carbohydrate, 0 g fiber, 360 mg sodium

MAKE-AHEAD: Sauce can be made 1 day in advance and refrigerated in a covered container until ready to use. If separation occurs, whisk before serving.

Barley and Mushroom "Risotto"

PREP TIME: 20 minutes   **COOK TIME:** 1 hour

Hearty, earthy flavors come together to create this creamy risotto-style dish that makes a perfect match with the beefy tenderloin. Here mushrooms play a dual role: Finely chopped, they round out the dish and complement the barley in shape and size; sliced, they provide visual contrast and extra flavor.

6 cups lower-sodium chicken broth	2 medium carrots, finely chopped
3 tablespoons extra-virgin olive oil	½ teaspoon dried thyme
1 large onion, finely chopped	½ teaspoon salt
3 celery stalks, finely diced	¼ teaspoon freshly ground black pepper
1 pound white mushrooms, finely chopped	1½ cups barley
¾ pound white mushrooms, sliced	1 bay leaf

Bring broth to a boil; remove from heat, cover, and set aside.

Heat oil in a large saucepan over medium heat. Add onion and cook until softened, 3 to 5 minutes. Add celery and cook until softened, about 5 minutes. Add mushrooms, carrots, thyme, salt, and pepper; cook until vegetables are softened and mushrooms have released their liquid, about 10 minutes. Add barley, bay leaf, and 2 cups of the reserved chicken broth. Increase heat to medium-high and simmer, stirring occasionally, until broth is almost absorbed, about 10 minutes.

Add remaining broth, ½ cup at a time, stirring frequently and waiting until broth is almost absorbed before adding more; do this until all broth is added and barley is tender, about 30 minutes. Discard bay leaf. Serve hot.

Makes 16 (½-cup) servings

NUTRITION AT A GLANCE
Per serving: 110 calories, 3 g fat, 0.5 g saturated fat, 5 g protein, 17 g carbohydrate, 4 g fiber, 300 mg sodium

MAKE-AHEAD: Risotto can be prepared up to 3 days in advance and refrigerated in a covered container until ready to use. To reheat, add ½ cup lower-sodium chicken broth or water, cover, and bake for 20 minutes at 350°F, stirring once.

Butternut Squash Purée

PREP TIME: 10 minutes   **COOK TIME: 55 minutes (including cooling time)**

Butternut squash adds gorgeous color to this holiday meal, but that's not all! This favorite veggie also provides great nutritional benefits, including ample amounts of beta-carotene and fiber, plus iron and vitamins B and E.

 2 (2-pound) butternut squash

 2 tablespoons extra-virgin olive oil

 ½ teaspoon dried thyme

 ¼ teaspoon salt

 ⅛ teaspoon freshly ground black pepper

 4 garlic cloves, unpeeled

Heat oven to 400°F. Line a baking pan with foil.

Cut squash in half lengthwise and scoop out seeds. Brush flesh side of squash with oil and season with thyme, salt, and pepper. Brush garlic with oil and place 1 clove in each of the squash cavities.

Transfer squash to baking pan and roast, cut side up, until skin is blistered and is easily pierced with a paring knife, 40 to 45 minutes. Remove from oven and cool for 10 minutes.

When cooled, scoop flesh from squash and transfer to a medium bowl. Squeeze garlic from the peel and mash with squash until garlic is incorporated and squash is smooth. Adjust seasonings to taste.

Makes 8 (¾-cup) servings

NUTRITION AT A GLANCE

Per serving: 110 calories, 3.5 g fat, 0.5 g saturated fat, 2 g protein, 21 g carbohydrate, 4 g fiber, 80 mg sodium

MAKE-AHEAD: Purée can be made up to 1 day in advance; store in a covered container in the refrigerator until ready to use. Heat through in a 325°F oven before serving.

Red and Green Leaf Salad with Champagne Vinaigrette

PREP TIME: 10 minutes

Two colorful lettuces keep the sentiment of the holiday alive in this simple salad. If you can't find champagne vinegar, choose a good-quality white wine vinegar.

 1 (½-pound) head red leaf lettuce

 1 (½-pound) head green leaf lettuce

 1½ tablespoons champagne vinegar

 1½ teaspoons Dijon mustard

 3 tablespoons extra-virgin olive oil

 1 tablespoon warm water

 1 shallot, minced

 Salt and freshly ground black pepper

Tear or chop the lettuce into bite-size pieces and place in a large serving bowl.

Whisk together vinegar and mustard in a small bowl. Slowly whisk in oil, then whisk in water and shallot. Season to taste with salt and pepper. Toss lettuce with dressing just before serving.

Makes 8 (2-cup) servings

NUTRITION AT A GLANCE
Per serving: 60 calories, 5 g fat, 0.5 g saturated fat, 1 g protein, 2 g carbohydrate, 1 g fiber, 40 mg sodium

MAKE-AHEAD: Dressing can be made up to 1 day in advance and refrigerated in a covered container. Bring to room temperature and whisk well before using.

Baked Pears with Chocolate Sauce and Pomegranate Seeds

PREP TIME: 10 minutes   **COOK TIME:** 1 hour

Juicy Anjou pears dress up for the best part of the party. They are widely available at Christmastime and are great for baking; you can also use Bosc, if you'd like.

4 Anjou pears, peeled, halved lengthwise, and cored

⅛ teaspoon ground cinnamon

1 tablespoon trans-fat-free margarine, cut into 8 pieces

⅓ cup water

½ cup bittersweet chocolate chips

2 tablespoons plus 1 teaspoon fat-free half-and-half

½ cup pomegranate seeds

Heat oven to 350°F. Sprinkle pears with cinnamon and place, cut side up, in a baking dish. Place 1 piece of margarine in the core cavity of each pear. Add water to dish and bake pears until tender, about 1 hour, basting with water once halfway through. Remove from oven and cool slightly. Slice each pear lengthwise into thin slices and fan out on dessert plates.

Heat chocolate and half-and-half in a small saucepan over medium-low heat, stirring constantly, until melted and well combined, 1 to 2 minutes. Using a large spoon, drizzle chocolate sauce decoratively over pear slices. Sprinkle with pomegranate seeds and serve.

Makes 8 servings

NUTRITION AT A GLANCE
Per serving: 120 calories, 4 g fat, 2 g saturated fat, 1 g protein, 24 g carbohydrate, 3 g fiber, 20 mg sodium

MAKE-AHEAD: Pomegranate can be seeded up to 3 days in advance and the seeds refrigerated in a covered container until ready to use. Pears can be baked 1 day in advance and refrigerated in a covered container. When ready to serve, heat pears in a 325°F oven until warmed through.

TIP **To avoid pomegranate stains:** When seeding a pomegranate, submerge the scored fruit in a large bowl of cold water and then gently pull the sections apart. The seeds will sink to the bottom, the membranes will float to the top, and your hands and clothes will remain clean.

CHRISTMAS DAY

FOR 4 GUESTS FOR BREAKFAST; 8 GUESTS FOR DINNER

The merriment of Christmas Day begins in the early morning hours for most of us, and nothing starts the festivities off better than holiday breakfast fare. Gorgeous egg soufflés will get energy flowing, and spiced tea, served with moist cranberry cake, will help keep it going right through the morning as you open presents and anticipate the fun to come.

Christmas dinner is a regal affair, with relatives and friends invited to join you mid- to late afternoon. The star of the meal is a stunning main course that's surprisingly simple to prepare: a crown roast of pork dressed in all of its finery. Fitting accompaniments include a beautiful dish of braised cabbage, a lovely plate of almond-coated green beans, and a nutritious pilaf made with wild rice. And for dessert, two special offerings—one fruit and one chocolate—add the perfect sweet touch to end this memorable holiday meal.

◀ *A beautiful crown roast acts as the centerpiece at this holiday table. Frosted pinecones and greens add pretty seasonal touches.*

MENU

WAKE-UP BREAKFAST
Egg, Pepper, and Scallion Soufflés
Whole-Grain Cranberry Spice Cake
Spiced Tea

CHRISTMAS DINNER
Crown Roast of Pork
Apple-Onion Chutney
Braised Red Cabbage
Green Beans Amandine
Wild Rice Pilaf
Mixed Green Salad with Pomegranate Vinaigrette
Chocolate, Almond, and Orange Clusters
Holiday Apple Crisp

Holiday Game Plan

Up to 1 month before: Make and freeze spice cake.

Up to 3 days before: Make chocolate clusters; order crown roast; toast almonds.

Up to 2 days before: Make chutney; prepare pilaf (except for parsley).

Up to 1 day before: Prepare ginger mixture for tea; braise cabbage; blanch green beans; make salad dressing; make crisp; thaw spice cake.

Day of: Make egg soufflés and tea; roast pork; finish green beans and pilaf; assemble salad; heat crisp.

Egg, Pepper, and Scallion Soufflés

PREP TIME: 10 minutes   COOK TIME: 30 minutes

This frittata-like breakfast soufflé is easy to prepare. The key is to serve it immediately, while piping hot and puffed up high. Make individual servings in 1-cup ramekins or custard cups and serve straight from the oven or use a 1½-quart soufflé dish (the cooking time won't vary). Heating the vegetables and eggs together before baking helps blend the flavors and speeds up the baking time.

    8 large eggs
    ⅓ cup reduced-fat sour cream
    ½ teaspoon salt
    ⅛ teaspoon freshly ground black pepper
    2 teaspoons trans-fat-free margarine
    1 small red bell pepper, diced
    ¼ cup sliced scallions

Position rack in middle of oven and heat oven to 350°F. Lightly coat 4 (1-cup) ramekins or custard cups with cooking spray.

Whisk together eggs, sour cream, salt, and black pepper in a large bowl.

Melt margarine in a large skillet over medium heat. Add bell pepper and scallions and cook until softened, about 3 minutes.

Pour egg mixture into skillet and cook, stirring frequently, until eggs have thickened slightly, 2 minutes. Divide mixture among the ramekins and bake until edges have puffed up and top is golden, about 25 minutes. Serve immediately, since soufflés will fall after a minute or so, or allow to fall, unmold, and serve on a platter.

Makes 4 servings

NUTRITION AT A GLANCE
Per serving: 200 calories, 14 g fat, 5 g saturated fat, 13 g protein, 3 g carbohydrate, 0 g fiber, 460 mg sodium

Whole-Grain Cranberry Spice Cake

PREP TIME: 20 minutes   **COOK TIME:** 1 hour   **COOLING TIME:** 10 minutes

A slice of this fruity, spiced breakfast bread is perfect with a hot cup of coffee or Spiced Tea (see opposite page) while you open the presents or enjoy the afternoon at home with friends and family. Freshly grated nutmeg adds a fresher, more pungent flavor than the ready-ground version; you'll find the whole spice in your market's spice section. Use a rasp or fine grater to grind just what you need.

1¾ cups whole-grain pastry flour	½ cup granular sugar substitute
1 teaspoon ground cinnamon	½ cup egg substitute
½ teaspoon freshly grated nutmeg	¼ cup extra-virgin olive oil
½ teaspoon baking powder	¾ teaspoon vanilla extract
¼ teaspoon baking soda	¼ teaspoon orange extract
⅛ teaspoon salt	1¾ cups fresh or frozen cranberries
1 cup fat-free milk	

Position rack in middle of oven and heat oven to 350°F. Lightly coat a 4 by 8 inch loaf pan with cooking spray.

Sift flour, cinnamon, nutmeg, baking powder, baking soda, and salt into a large bowl. Make a well in the center of the dry ingredients.

In a medium bowl, whisk together milk, sugar substitute, egg substitute, oil, and vanilla and orange extracts. Add the wet ingredients to the dry ingredients; stir well to combine. Fold in cranberries. Spoon batter into loaf pan, spreading evenly.

Bake until a tester inserted in the center comes out clean, about 1 hour. Cool in pan on rack for 10 minutes, then turn cake out onto rack to cool completely before serving.

Makes 12 slices

NUTRITION AT A GLANCE

Per slice: 150 calories, 5 g fat, 0.5 g saturated fat, 4 g protein, 22 g carbohydrate, 3 g fiber, 125 mg sodium

MAKE-AHEAD: Cake can be made up to 4 days in advance, wrapped in foil, and refrigerated. Bring to room temperature before serving. Or it can be frozen for up to 1 month; defrost at room temperature.

Spiced Tea

PREP TIME: 10 minutes   **COOK TIME:** 40 minutes   **STEEPING TIME:** 30 minutes or overnight

Cinnamon, cloves, ginger, and peppercorns create a warming tea that fills the house with a tantalizing scent. Kept warm in a thermos, the tea will be at-the-ready for family members and any surprise visitors. Serve the tea with fat-free or low-fat milk or fat-free half-and-half for a beverage that's like chai, the beloved spice milk tea from India that has become a worldwide favorite.

- 9 cups water
- 2 tablespoons roughly chopped fresh ginger
- 2 cinnamon sticks
- ¼ teaspoon whole cloves
- ¼ teaspoon black peppercorns
- 3 (1-inch) strips lemon zest
- 3 (1-inch) strips orange zest
- 10 caffeinated or decaffeinated black tea bags
- 3 tablespoons granular sugar substitute (optional)

Bring water to a boil in a large saucepan. Add ginger, cinnamon, cloves, peppercorns, and zests. Reduce heat to low and simmer gently, uncovered, for 30 minutes. Remove from heat and allow to steep at room temperature for 30 minutes or in the refrigerator overnight.

When ready to serve, return ginger mixture to a boil. Remove from heat, add tea bags, cover, and steep for 5 minutes. Squeeze tea bags into liquid, then strain and discard solids. Add sugar substitute for a sweeter tea, if desired, and serve hot.

Makes 8 (¾-cup) drinks

NUTRITION AT A GLANCE

Per drink: 0 calories, 0 g fat, 0 g saturated fat, 0 g protein, 0 g carbohydrate, 0 g fiber, 0 mg sodium

MAKE-AHEAD: Ginger mixture can be prepared up to 1 day in advance and stored in a covered container in the refrigerator. Add the tea bags and steep the tea right before serving.

Crown Roast of Pork

PREP TIME: 15 minutes   **MARINATING TIME:** 8 hours or overnight
COOK TIME: 2 hours   **RESTING TIME:** 20 minutes

This regal dish is easy to make. Ask the butcher to trim the fat, french the bones to expose the tips, and tie the rack into a crown.

2 tablespoons plus 2 teaspoons extra-virgin olive oil

2 garlic cloves, minced

2 tablespoons chopped fresh sage

2 tablespoons chopped fresh oregano or 2 teaspoons dried oregano

½ teaspoon freshly ground black pepper

¼ teaspoon salt

1 (6- to 7-pound) crown roast of pork, fat trimmed and bones frenched

4 celery stalks, cut into 1½-inch pieces

2 medium onions, quartered

2 medium carrots, cut into 1½-inch pieces

¼ cup plus 2 tablespoons water

¼ cup red wine

Whisk together 2 teaspoons of the oil, garlic, sage, oregano, pepper, and salt in a small bowl. Rub pork all over with garlic mixture. Cover pork with plastic wrap and refrigerate for 8 hours or overnight.

Position rack in lower third of oven and heat oven to 425°F.

Toss celery, onions, and carrots with remaining 2 tablespoons oil in a roasting pan; set pork on top. Wrap bone tips with foil to prevent burning.

Roast pork for 30 minutes, reduce heat to 350°F, and continue roasting, turning pan halfway through, until thermometer inserted in thickest part of a few of the chops reads 155° to 160°F, 1¼ to 1½ hours.

Remove roast from oven and remove foil from bone tips. Carefully transfer roast to a platter, loosely cover with foil, and let rest for 20 minutes.

While roast is resting, remove vegetables from pan and discard. Place roasting pan over low heat and add water and wine. Bring to a simmer and, using a wooden spoon, scrape browned bits of pork from bottom of the pan. Simmer until you have a flavorful juice, 3 to 4 minutes.

Carve roast into thick chops and serve with pan juices.

Makes 16 to 20 chops

NUTRITION AT A GLANCE
Per chop: 170 calories, 9 g fat, 2.5 g saturated fat, 19 g protein, 0 g carbohydrate, 0 g fiber, 75 mg sodium

Apple-Onion Chutney

PREP TIME: 10 minutes   **COOK TIME:** 35 minutes

This sweet and vinegary condiment is the perfect complement to pork, ham, or chicken. Leaving the peel on the apples adds fiber. Serve it in a pretty bowl with a special serving spoon or in the crown of the roast.

6   cups unsweetened apple cider

5   medium white onions or sweet onions (such as Vidalia), quartered

½   cup cider vinegar

1   tablespoon granular sugar substitute

1   tablespoon minced fresh ginger

3   large Granny Smith apples, diced

Pinch of ground cinnamon or ground cloves

¼   teaspoon salt

Pinch of freshly ground black pepper

Combine cider, onions, vinegar, sugar substitute, and ginger in a large saucepan. Bring mixture to a boil, reduce heat to a simmer, and cook, stirring occasionally, until the liquid is reduced to a syrupy consistency, 20 to 25 minutes.

Stir in apples, cinnamon, salt, and pepper. Continue to simmer gently until fruit is soft and chutney is thickened, 5 to 10 minutes. Serve warm or at room temperature.

Makes 2 cups

NUTRITION AT A GLANCE

Per tablespoon: 35 calories, 0 g fat, 0 g saturated fat, 0 g protein, 9 g carbohydrate, 3 g fiber, 25 mg sodium

MAKE-AHEAD: The entire recipe can be made up to 2 days in advance; keep chutney refrigerated in a covered container until ready to serve.

Braised Red Cabbage

PREP TIME: 10 minutes   **COOK TIME:** 1 hour 5 minutes

The ruby red hue of this colorful cruciferous vegetable contrasts beautifully with the green beans at this elegant Christmas meal. Although all cabbage contains vitamin C, the red variety packs the most, providing nearly two-thirds of the recommended daily allowance in a 1-cup serving. If you have a food processor, use the grating attachment for easy cabbage shredding.

> 2 teaspoons extra-virgin olive oil
> 1 small onion, chopped
> 1 medium (2-pound) head red cabbage, thinly sliced (about 8 cups)
> ⅓ cup lower-sodium chicken broth
> 3 tablespoons red wine vinegar
> 1 teaspoon caraway seeds (optional)
>   Salt and freshly ground black pepper

Heat oil over medium heat in a large nonstick saucepan. Add onion and cook until softened, about 5 minutes. Stir in cabbage, broth, vinegar, and caraway seeds, if using. Bring mixture to a simmer, cover, reduce heat to low, and cook until cabbage is very soft, about 1 hour. Season to taste with salt and pepper. Serve warm.

Makes 8 (1-cup) servings

NUTRITION AT A GLANCE
Per serving: 40 calories, 1.5 g fat, 0 g saturated fat, 1 g protein, 7 g carbohydrate, 2 g fiber, 45 mg sodium

MAKE-AHEAD: Cabbage can be braised up to 1 day in advance and stored in a covered container in the refrigerator. Reheat in a microwave or on the stove top before serving.

Green Beans Amandine

PREP TIME: 15 minutes   **COOK TIME:** 20 minutes

Garlic and toasted slivered almonds make ordinary green beans extra special. Prepare the beans in batches if you do not have a large enough skillet, keeping the first round warm until the second batch is ready.

- ½ cup slivered almonds
- 2 pounds green beans, trimmed
- 1 tablespoon extra-virgin olive oil
- 6 garlic cloves, thinly sliced
- ¼ teaspoon salt
-    Freshly ground black pepper

Heat oven to 275°F. Spread almonds on a baking sheet and toast, stirring once, until fragrant and golden, about 10 minutes. Transfer to a plate to cool.

While almonds are toasting, bring a large saucepan of water to a boil. Add beans and cook just until crisp-tender, about 3 minutes. Drain in a colander and run under very cold water for 1 minute to stop cooking. Drain again and pat dry.

Heat oil in a large nonstick skillet over medium heat. Add garlic, reduce heat to medium-low, and cook, stirring frequently, until garlic is lightly golden and fragrant, about 2 minutes. Add beans and toss well to coat. Cover pan, increase heat to high, and cook until beans are heated through, 2 to 3 minutes. Transfer beans to a serving bowl and toss with almonds, salt, and pepper to taste. Serve warm.

Makes 8 (1-cup) servings

NUTRITION AT A GLANCE
Per serving: 80 calories, 5 g fat, 0.5 g saturated fat, 3 g protein, 9 g carbohydrate, 5 g fiber, 75 mg sodium

MAKE-AHEAD: Almond slices can be toasted up to 3 days ahead; store in a covered container in the refrigerator. Cook beans and pat dry up to 1 day in advance. Store refrigerated in a covered container until ready to use. Finish final step before serving.

Wild Rice Pilaf

PREP TIME: 8 minutes   **COOK TIME:** 1 hour

Wild rice, actually a type of grass, has twice the amount of protein as traditional white or brown rice. Cooking it in chicken broth adds rich flavor to the dish, but you can use water or vegetable broth if you prefer.

- 2 cups lower-sodium chicken broth
- ¾ cup wild rice
- 2 teaspoons extra-virgin olive oil
- 1 small onion, finely chopped
- 2 celery stalks, finely chopped
- 1 small Granny Smith apple, finely chopped
- ½ teaspoon dried thyme
  Salt and freshly ground black pepper
- ¼ cup chopped fresh parsley

Bring broth to a boil in a medium saucepan. Stir in rice, cover, and cook over low heat until tender, about 45 minutes. Drain any extra liquid after rice has cooked. Set aside.

Heat oil in a large nonstick skillet over medium heat. Add onion and cook until softened, about 5 minutes. Add celery and cook 5 minutes more. Stir in apple and thyme; cook 3 minutes more. Stir in reserved rice and cook just until heated through. Season to taste with salt and pepper. Stir in parsley and serve warm.

Makes 16 (½-cup) servings

NUTRITION AT A GLANCE
Per serving: 80 calories, 1.5 g fat, 0 g saturated fat, 3 g protein, 15 g carbohydrate, 2 g fiber, 150 mg sodium

MAKE-AHEAD: You can prepare the rice up to 2 days in advance; don't add the parsley. Reheat in a microwave and stir in the parsley just before serving.

Mixed Green Salad with Pomegranate Vinaigrette

PREP TIME: 25 minutes

This lovely seasonal salad arrives at the table practically sparkling with juicy, deep-red pomegranate seeds. Shallots in the vinaigrette add an understated elegance. See page 215 for a tip on how to seed pomegranates easily without getting stained.

1 pound mixed baby greens (16 cups)

1 medium fennel bulb, thinly sliced

¾ cup pomegranate seeds

3 tablespoons extra-virgin olive oil

1 tablespoon plus 1 teaspoon fresh lemon juice

1 tablespoon minced shallot or red onion

1 teaspoon grated lemon zest

Salt and freshly ground black pepper

Toss together greens, fennel, and pomegranate seeds in a large bowl.

Whisk together oil, lemon juice, shallot, zest, and a pinch of salt in a small bowl. Allow dressing to sit for at least 10 minutes.

Just before serving, whisk dressing, pour over greens, and toss gently. Season with salt and pepper to taste, and serve.

Makes 8 (2-cup) servings

NUTRITION AT A GLANCE
Per serving: 80 calories, 6 g fat, 0.5 g saturated fat, 2 g protein, 7 g carbohydrate, 2 g fiber, 0 mg sodium

MAKE-AHEAD: Dressing can be made up to 1 day ahead and refrigerated in a covered container. Bring to room temperature and whisk well before serving.

Chocolate, Almond, and Orange Clusters

PREP TIME: 5 minutes   **COOK TIME:** 10 minutes   **FREEZING TIME:** 45 minutes

Sweet fruit, freshly toasted nuts, and rich chocolate are an unparalleled trio in these delectable cookies. Send extras home with your guests, in cellophane bags tied with festive holiday ribbon. You might also want to make the Almond Star Cookies (page 184) for this meal. You can use any shape Christmas cookie cutters you like.

- 2   cups whole almonds
- ½   cup bittersweet chocolate chips
- ¼   cup fat-free half-and-half
- 2   teaspoons vanilla extract
- 1   teaspoon finely grated orange zest

Heat oven to 350°F. Place almonds on a baking sheet and toast until fragrant and lightly golden, 6 to 8 minutes. Remove from oven and cool. When cool, chop coarsely and set aside.

Line a baking sheet with wax paper or parchment.

Combine chocolate chips, half-and-half, and vanilla in a small saucepan. Stirring constantly, cook over low heat until chips are melted and mixture is smooth, 2 to 3 minutes. Remove from the heat and add zest and almonds. Stir to coat well.

Drop by the tablespoon onto the baking sheet. Freeze on the sheet until set, at least 45 minutes. Transfer to a platter and serve immediately.

Makes 24 clusters

NUTRITION AT A GLANCE
Per cluster: 90 calories, 7 g fat, 1 g saturated fat, 3 g protein, 5 g carbohydrate, 1 g fiber, 0 mg sodium

MAKE-AHEAD: Clusters can be made up to 3 days in advance. After freezing for 45 minutes, refrigerate in a covered container until ready to serve.

Holiday Apple Crisp

PREP TIME: 20 minutes   **COOK TIME:** 45 minutes

Warm and fruity, this seemingly familiar apple crisp is spiked with sweet and tangy dried cherries. Fresh or dried, cherries contain impressive amounts of antioxidants, as well as soluble fiber and potassium. Ounce for ounce, dried cherries are higher in nutrients than their fresh counterparts, but they also have more calories. So it's best to enjoy them in moderation, as you will here.

¼ cup unsweetened dried cherries

½ cup water

½ cup old-fashioned rolled oats

½ cup trans-fat-free margarine

½ cup whole-grain pastry flour

¼ cup plus 2 tablespoons granular sugar substitute

2 tablespoons ground cinnamon

9 Granny Smith apples, sliced (9 to 10 cups)

2 tablespoons fresh lemon juice

Preheat oven to 350°F. Lightly coat a 9- by 13-inch baking dish with cooking spray.

Place cherries and water in a bowl and soak cherries until ready to use.

Meanwhile, combine oats, margarine, ¼ cup of the flour, ¼ cup of the sugar substitute, and 1 tablespoon of the cinnamon in a medium bowl; stir until mixture is crumbly.

Toss apples and lemon juice together in a large bowl. Add remaining ¼ cup flour, 2 tablespoons sugar substitute, and remaining 1 tablespoon cinnamon; stir to combine.

Place apples in baking dish. Pour cherries and soaking water over apple mixture; toss gently to combine. Sprinkle oat topping evenly over fruit. Bake until apples are tender, about 40 minutes. Serve warm.

Makes 12 (1-cup) servings

NUTRITION AT A GLANCE
Per serving: 150 calories, 7 g fat, 2 g saturated fat, 1 g protein, 23 g carbohydrate, 5 g fiber, 60 mg sodium

MAKE-AHEAD: Crisp can be made up to 1 day in advance. Cool completely in the baking dish, then cover and refrigerate. Heat through in a 325°F oven before serving.

INDEX

Underscored page references indicate boxed text or tips. **Boldfaced** page references indicate photographs.

Strawberries
    Chocolate-Dipped Strawberries, 96
    Star-Spangled Berries, 183
    Strawberry Blancmange, **132,** 133
    Strawberry-Limeade Sparklers, 185
Stuffing
    Turkey Sausage and Pear Stuffing, 190
Sunflower seeds
    Green Salad with Mushrooms and Sunflower
        Seeds, 117
Sweet potatoes
    Cider-Roasted Sweet Potatoes, 192–93
    Sweet Potato and Zucchini Latkes, **202,** 203
    Sweet Potato–Feta Rounds, 95
Swiss chard
    Ruby Swiss Chard Sauté, 129
    stems, chopping and cooking, 129

T

Tacos
    Soft Chicken Tacos, 160, **161**
Tahini
    Tahini Dip with Veggies, 200
Tartlets
    Cannoli Tartlets, 97
Tea
    Spiced Tea, 221
Tomatoes
    Baked Tomatoes with Feta and Herbs, 130
    Broccolini with Warm Sun-Dried Tomato
        Vinaigrette, **173,** 174
    Caprese Skewers, 15
    Endive Spears with Fresh Pepper Salsa, 156
    Fresh Tomato Salad, 178
    Panzanella Salad, 63
    Penne with Homemade Tomato Sauce, 30
    Roasted Pepper Gazpacho, 80
    Roasted Zucchini Bites, 146, **147**
    Smoked Trout Salad in Cherry Tomato Cups,
        90
    Squash and Tomato Tian, 141
    storing, 178
    Sun-Dried Tomato Hummus, 52
    Turkey Pasta Diablo, 197
Tortillas
    Soft Chicken Tacos, 160, **161**
Trout
    Smoked Trout Salad in Cherry Tomato Cups,
        90
Tuna
    Italian Tuna Salad Bites, 103
    Zesty Salad Niçoise, 48
Turkey
    Curried Turkey Salad, 197
    Ginger Turkey Stir-Fry, 197

leftover, serving ideas, 197
Mexican Turkey Scramble, 197
Roast Turkey with Fresh Herbs, 188–89
Turkey and Watercress Tea Sandwiches, 36
Turkey Chili, 196
Turkey Pasta Diablo, 197
Turkey Sausage and Pear Stuffing, 190
whole, carving, 189

V

Vegetables. *See also specific types*
    Crudités with Arugula Pesto Dip, 34
    Grilled Vegetable Skewers, 82–83, **83**
    in Phase 2, xii
    Tahini Dip with Veggies, 200

W

Walnuts
    Chocolate-Dipped Strawberries, 96
    Endive Spears with Walnut Goat Cheese, 70
    Haroset, 136
    Holiday Spiced Nuts, 209
    South Beach Waldorf Salad, 29
Watercress
    Guacamole Salad, 158
    Turkey and Watercress Tea Sandwiches, 36
Water intake, 6
Weight loss, xii, xiii
Wild rice
    Wild Rice Pilaf, 227
Wine, xii, 3, 6

Y

Yogurt
    Banana-Orange Pops, 31
    Blueberry-Melon Smoothies, 49
    Cucumber Sticks with Tzatziki Dip, 14
    Curried Chicken Skewers with Yogurt Dip,
        102
    Grilled Shrimp with Chipotle Dip, 157
    Salmon Mousse, 93
    Tahini Dip with Veggies, 200

Z

Zucchini
    Grilled Vegetable Skewers, 82–83, **83**
    Parmesan Zucchini Sticks, 94
    Roasted Zucchini Bites, 146, **147**
    Squash and Tomato Tian, 141
    Sweet Potato and Zucchini Latkes, **202,**
        203
    Zucchini Soup with Basil Cream, 169

Conversion Chart

These equivalents have been slightly rounded to make measuring easier.

Volume Measurements

U.S.	Imperial	Metric
¼ tsp	–	1 ml
½ tsp	–	2 ml
1 tsp	–	5 ml
1 Tbsp	–	15 ml
2 Tbsp (1 oz)	1 fl oz	30 ml
¼ cup (2 oz)	2 fl oz	60 ml
⅓ cup (3 oz)	3 fl oz	80 ml
½ cup (4 oz)	4 fl oz	120 ml
⅔ cup (5 oz)	5 fl oz	160 ml
¾ cup (6 oz)	6 fl oz	180 ml
1 cup (8 oz)	8 fl oz	240 ml

Weight Measurements

U.S.	Metric
1 oz	30 g
2 oz	60 g
4 oz (¼ lb)	115 g
5 oz (⅓ lb)	145 g
6 oz	170 g
7 oz	200 g
8 oz (½ lb)	230 g
10 oz	285 g
12 oz (¾ lb)	340 g
14 oz	400 g
16 oz (1 lb)	455 g
2.2 lb	1 kg

Length Measurements

U.S.	Metric
¼"	0.6 cm
½"	1.25 cm
1"	2.5 cm
2"	5 cm
4"	11 cm
6"	15 cm
8"	20 cm
10"	25 cm
12" (1')	30 cm

Pan Sizes

U.S.	Metric
8" cake pan	20 × 4 cm sandwich or cake tin
9" cake pan	23 × 3.5 cm sandwich or cake tin
11" × 7" baking pan	28 × 18 cm baking tin
13" × 9" baking pan	32.5 × 23 cm baking tin
15" × 10" baking pan	38 × 25.5 cm baking tin (Swiss roll tin)
1½ qt baking dish	1.5 liter baking dish
2 qt baking dish	2 liter baking dish
2 qt rectangular baking dish	30 × 19 cm baking dish
9" pie plate	22 × 4 or 23 × 4 cm pie plate
7" or 8" springform pan	18 or 20 cm springform or loose-bottom cake tin
9" × 5" loaf pan	23 × 13 cm or 2 lb narrow loaf tin or pâté tin

Temperatures

Fahrenheit	Centigrade	Gas
140°	60°	–
160°	70°	–
180°	80°	–
225°	105°	¼
250°	120°	½
275°	135°	1
300°	150°	2
325°	160°	3
350°	180°	4
375°	190°	5
400°	200°	6
425°	220°	7
450°	230°	8
475°	245°	9
500°	260°	–